Reimagining Fairness: The Equity, Cultural Diversity, & Inclusion Competency Approach

A sustainable approach for adapting to and thriving in the era of balancing legal risks and marketplace opportunities

By Billy E. Vaughn, Ph.D.
DTUI.com

For permission requests, contact the publisher at:

Diversity Training University International (DTUI.com LLC)
San Francisco, CA
www.dtui.com

First Edition: 2025
ISBN: 979-8-9991437-0-9

Cover design by Imran Lodhi
Interior layout by DTUI.com Publishing

Printed in the United States of America
First Edition
Library of Congress Control Number: [In progress]

www.dtui.com

Praise for Reimagining Fairness and Dr. Billy E. Vaughn

"There may not be a timelier and more needed book than this one which connects diversity, inclusion, and cultural change with business strategy. Billy Vaughn makes the value of the strategic connection clear and shows the essential steps to getting the work done in organizations."
– Gerald Harris, Author of The Art of Quantum Planning, Scenario Planning Futurist

"Dr. Billy Vaughn's Reimagining Fairness is a timely and invaluable guide for navigating today's complex DEIBA landscape. With a rich historical lens and forward-thinking strategies, this book offers essential insights for driving workplace transformation. A must-read for leaders committed to diversity, equity, inclusion, and meaningful change—especially in the current climate."
– Dr. Edward E. Hubbard, Founder of Diversity ROI Measurement/Analytic Sciences; President/CEO, Hubbard & Hubbard, Inc.

"In Reimagining Fairness, Billy introduces the Equity, Cultural Diversity, and Inclusion (ECDI) Competency Approach, a practical, clear roadmap for leaders and practitioners ready to move beyond quick fixes and build workplaces rooted in real equity—the kind that can withstand political pressure and legal scrutiny without losing their soul. This isn't a book about guilt or performative gestures. It's about making fairness part of how your organization actually works. If you care about building a culture where everyone has a real chance to succeed, this book is for you."
– Dr. J. Bruce Stewart, CEO, The Small World Solutions Group; Author of The Click Code: Why Some Teams Click and Some Don't and The Race Ahead: Overcoming Racial Bias by Rewiring the American Mind

"In an era marked by rapid change and deep polarization, this book offers a powerful and practical guide for organizations committed to driving systemic, lasting change. It lays out a blueprint to build fair, equitable workplaces where every individual's talent is recognized, valued, and unleashed. A must-read for anyone serious about transforming their organization for the better."
– Judith H. Katz, Ed.D., Executive Vice President, Emerita, The Kaleel Jamison Consulting Group, Inc.; Author of The Power of Agency: Cultivating Autonomy, Authority and Leadership in Every Role

Acknowledgements

I offer my deepest gratitude to those who have guided, supported, and inspired me throughout my personal and professional journey.

To my beloved, late maternal grandmother, Annie Naomi Barzeron, thank you for embodying compassion and modeling the true meaning of care, strength, and resilience. Your legacy continues to shape who I am.

To Judith Katz, Ed.D. Your example, generosity as a mentor, and unwavering encouragement have been a beacon throughout my career. I am profoundly grateful for the wisdom and inspiration you've so selflessly shared.

To Raymond Trybus, Ph.D. I appreciate your thoughtful guidance and steadfast support in my professional growth. Your mentorship has helped me face challenges with confidence and clarity.

I also extend heartfelt thanks to the Diversity Executive Leadership Academy advisory board. Your belief in me and in the mission of DTUI.com has been essential to our shared success. Your advocacy and commitment have left an enduring impact.

To each of you, thank you for walking this journey with me. Your contributions have been invaluable.

Table of Contents

Preface

For decades, organizations have grappled with designing, developing, and implementing high-impact diversity, equity, and inclusion (DEI) initiatives that create meaningful and measurable impact with the least pushback. Too often, these efforts become cycles of well-intentioned but ineffective programs that fail to dismantle systemic barriers. While diversity best practices offer valuable guidance, many organizations mistakenly treat them as one-size-fits-all solutions rather than embedding them within a strategic organizational change framework. This oversight limits their effectiveness and strengthens opposition to DEI's legitimacy.

The recent backlash against DEI has exposed a longstanding shortcoming in many initiatives, one that seasoned practitioners have warned about for years. Poorly conceived programs lack an organizational change strategy, legal jeopardy foresight, and long-term sustainability planning. As a result, DEI has demonstrated its power in achieving intended outcomes but has often failed to drive profound cultural change. Worse, rushed or ill-conceived practices have placed organizations in avoidable legal jeopardy, providing opponents with ample ammunition to challenge DEI as exclusionary or legally unsound.

Traditional DEI approaches often lag behind legal and political shifts, making them outdated in a rapidly evolving world. This underscores the urgency of rethinking practices and mindsets to build truly equitable organizations. Innovative DEI practitioners face key challenges, especially when challenging traditional values. They must think like organizational change agents and manage resistance to change while continuing to counter bias and attacks on DEI and integrate DEI into an organization's mission and operations.

The book introduces the Equity, Cultural Diversity, and Inclusion Competency (ECDI) approach to organizational culture change. Its focus is on cultural transformation, which goes beyond the popular DEI models. It emphasizes developing equity and inclusion competency and removing systemic equity barriers to align cultural diversity and inclusion efforts with business goals and legal standards.

This book urges DEI practitioners, organizational leaders, legal professionals, business leaders, equal employment opportunity professionals, and human resource managers to rethink their diversity, equity, and inclusion approach to enhance organizational success and mitigate risk. Instead of relying solely on borrowed best practices, organizations must adopt a strategic approach that integrates equity and inclusion into their talent management strategy while complying with legal constraints. Tackling these challenges directly can pave the way for a more culturally diverse, inclusive, and equitable organization that is better managed.

Each profession has specialized terminology and acronyms, and this book is no different. For the reader's convenience, keywords and definitions of terms are provided at the back of the book.

Billy E. Vaughn, PhD
Diversity Training University International (DTUI.com)
May 2025

Introduction

On May 25, 2020, George Floyd's demise in police custody was captured on video and broadcast around the world. This footage underscored law enforcement's history of disproportionately using force against Black American citizens. A police officer was recorded kneeling on George Floyd's neck for an extended period. Floyd died from "cardiopulmonary arrest" resulting from illegal "law enforcement subdual, restraint, and compression of the neck." The incident highlighted the deep-seated systemic issues that continue to perpetuate unfairness, oppression, and discrimination, igniting widespread outrage and leading to a global movement against racial injustice and police brutality. It also revealed America's lingering racial injustice and underscored the urgent need to address long-standing institutionalized racial inequity. As a result, George Floyd's tragic death in police custody heightened interest in achieving a more just American society.

Following Floyd's death, protests erupted worldwide, with millions of people taking to the streets in protest to demand justice and end racial discrimination. The scale and diversity among the protestors demonstrated that the injustice was not just a localized issue but a universal concern for humanity. It united people from different backgrounds, nationalities, races, and ethnicities internationally under the common cause of fighting for equality and justice. The widespread use of social media platforms allowed factual and counterfactual information, videos, and personal stories about racial injustice to go viral. Social media was crucial in mobilizing and organizing these protests, creating spaces for dialogue and education on diversity, inclusion, and equity issues. It amplified marginalized voices, enabling individuals to share their experiences and shed greater light on the everyday struggles that historically marginalized and excluded group communities face in encounters with the police.

In response to this public outcry, many corporations, organizations, and other institutions publicly acknowledged the need to address lingering racial injustice and increase efforts to promote DEI. Companies publicly announced statements of solidarity with the protests' mission, implemented diversity and inclusion initiatives, hired DEI practitioners for the first time, and pledged their financial support to social justice causes. This increased focus on DEI across sectors increased conversations about its need and brought the issues it addresses into the mainstream discourse.

The calls for justice and accountability renewed discussions about police reform, criminal justice reform, and broader policy changes to address racial disparities. Lawmakers at different levels of government proposed reforms such as enhanced police training, increased accountability measures, and efforts to dismantle systemic inequities embedded in policies and lines of authority. Numerous local, state, county, and city governments, led by progressive leaders, established racial equity initiatives and mandates. These actions generated greater interest in implementing DEI and recruiting professionals to manage the programs and initiatives. They also encouraged individuals, communities, organizations, and governments to reflect on their roles in promoting greater equality. This spurred a broader acknowledgment of the need for change and a commitment to fostering a more inclusive and equitable society.

Organizations with limited DEI programs recruited practitioners, often by reassigning employees, to work toward increasing workforce cultural diversity and fostering a more welcoming work environment. This heightened attention to addressing longstanding, institutionalized racial injustice and inequities underscored the limited impact of decades of legislation, mandates, policies, and "best practices" aimed at tackling these challenges.

Recent data indicate that many organizations publicly supporting social justice to uplift their brands failed to support that commitment with actionable efforts or plans. Many other organizations, including the recently recruited diversity practitioners, curtailed or eliminated their programs and initiatives. Consider the Equal Employment Opportunity Commission (EEOC) 2024 case against Morton Salt that involved a complaint by Daryl Dorsey, a Black American employee who alleged racial discrimination. The company reportedly committed to racial equity and social justice in 2020 after the George Floyd protests heated up. Dorsey claimed he faced a racially hostile work environment, was denied promotions, and was treated less favorably than his White American colleagues. The employee who trained him had a history of open racial hostility, which at one point led to the employee being fired, only to be rehired a couple of weeks later.

This case highlights the critical importance of aligning organizational practices with public commitments to DEI. It reminds us that genuine commitment requires more than statements. It necessitates consistent, proactive efforts to address and prevent discrimination in the workplace.

The Morton Salt case is a cautionary tale for companies that commit publicly to DEI solutions but fail to reflect them in their internal policies, procedures, and practices. When organizations publicly affirm their dedication to diversity and inclusion, they are not legally protected if their actions break the law. The case underscores the importance of developing and implementing a comprehensive DEI initiative after a public commitment. The message is clear: companies must move beyond performative gestures and commit to well-tested DEI best practices that are substantial, consistent, and lead to meaningful, measurable change. Otherwise, they risk legal action and damage to their credibility.

The surge of companies hiring DEI practitioners has sharply declined since the Supreme Court's June 2023 ruling against Harvard's use of race in admissions. Media coverage of conservative, anti-affirmative action groups fueled backlash, leading some states to ban support for DEI offices and programs. Many organizations retreated, exposing the performative nature of their prior commitments. In contrast, companies with deep, longstanding DEI efforts have largely stayed the course, recognizing the ongoing return on investment despite new risks.

DEI roles have notably decreased. By late 2022, turnover among DEI professionals reached 33%, exceeding other roles. Major companies like Amazon, Applebee's, Walmart, and X (formerly Twitter) cut or eliminated DEI teams. Meta discontinued its DEI programs, citing divisiveness. VP of HR Janelle Gale noted the term "DEI" had become negatively associated with preferential treatment. Government defunding and legal threats further chilled DEI momentum.

The inauguration of the 2024 Republican administration was soon afterwards followed by an intensified backlash, issuing executive orders targeting federal DEI-related programs, even challenging affirmative action. This quick retreat of organizations from commitments in the hostile anti-DEI environment raised doubts about the authenticity of their publicly stated social responsibility statements, leaving DEI practitioners questioning whether these efforts were ever more than PR strategies. Still, most organizations remain reluctant to abandon DEI entirely, given its value for inclusion and market reach.

A February 2024 Littler Mendelson PC survey of 320 C-suite executives found that 53% maintained DEI efforts, 17% increased them, and 69% said Supreme Court rulings hadn't changed their approach (Littler Mendelson PC, 2025). Only 1% reported a significant drop in commitment. Employee expectations concerning commitment to DEI were a significant decision-making factor. Shareholders at companies like Costco, Apple, John Deere, Disney, Levi Strauss, and Berkshire Hathaway overwhelmingly voted to sustain DEI, resisting conservative activist pressure. A vote against DEI was presumably considered a vote against their investment interests. More than 40% of companies with longstanding DEI programs have merely adjusted their practices to align with the Supreme Court decision, rather than addressing anti-DEI activism.

The market demands it. Younger job seekers prioritize diversity and inclusion; one-third of candidates from historically excluded groups won't apply to non-diverse companies. Glassdoor reports that 76% of job seekers rate workplace diversity as critical. ManpowerGroup found 68% of Gen Z workers dissatisfied with their employer's DEI efforts, while 70–80% of U.S. business leaders see DEI as core to business strategy, regardless of politics.

Talent retention is a key driver. Inclusive workplaces foster fairness, respect, and opportunity, boosting recruitment, engagement, and performance. Diverse teams outperform homogeneous ones in decision-making, innovation, and financial results. Research shows these gains require intentional efforts to build equitable environments where everyone can fully contribute (Hunt et al., 2020). Strong DEI practices also enhance public trust, customer loyalty, and brand reputation. Stakeholders expect businesses to demonstrate fairness and social responsibility (Glassdoor Team, 2020).

In summary, a culturally diverse, equitable, and inclusive workplace strengthens recruitment, retention, innovation, competitiveness, and trust. This makes DEI critical to long-term organizational success. Despite political and legal challenges, most companies remain committed, recognizing that abandoning DEI risks undermining both talent strategy and business outcomes (Gomez & Bernet, 2019).

For decades, organizations have struggled to implement high-impact diversity, equity, and inclusion (DEI) initiatives that create meaningful, measurable change. Too often, these efforts rely on one-size-fits-all best practices rather than strategic, systemic transformation. As a result, many initiatives fail to dismantle structural barriers, lack legal foresight, and leave organizations vulnerable to controversy and resistance.

The growing backlash against DEI underscores the flaws that few practitioners have long warned us about. Popular DEI approaches lag behind legal and political shifts, making them ineffective in today's complex business and regulatory landscape. Organizations must embed DEI into their core strategy to drive lasting change, anticipate legal challenges, and transform organizational culture beyond surface-level solutions. But how did DEI become a pariah, given its emphasis on inclusion and how can it continue to survive the lingering attacks and calls among practitioners to retreat?

The initials, DEI, represent an effort to address talent management challenges due to demographic shifts. They are not meant to reflect what the work is all about, nor its impact. Evidence supports that well-implemented DEI initiatives can enhance business performance, greater innovation, improved employee satisfaction, and better educational outcomes (Gomez, L. E., & Bernet, P., 2019). Organizations aiming to realize these benefits should focus on integrating DEI into their core operations and fostering an inclusive culture (Hunt, V., Prince, S., Dixon-Fyle, S., & Yee, L., 2020). But it is not enough to address the questions about what DEI is and means. We need a better understanding of the political, social, and economic environment, as well as the history of promoting equity, to devise a strategy for managing the inevitable turbulence and hostility due to competing cultural diversity-related agendas.

This book, Fairness Reimagined: The Equity, Cultural Diversity, and Inclusion Competency Approach, covers the current and historical context of implementing cultural diversity initiatives in introducing a unique approach to organizational culture change: the Equity, Cultural Diversity, and Inclusion Competency culture change framework. Unlike traditional DEI models focused on recruitment, representation, and equal pay, ECDI prioritizes cultural transformation as the foundation for sustainable equity. It emphasizes developing equity and inclusion competency (IEC) and removing systemic barriers, ensuring that DEI efforts align with business and organizational goals and legal standards while fostering genuine workplace inclusion.

Structured as a practical philosophy about how to lead cultural diversity initiatives and a practical guide, the book covers:

- The evolution of DEI, including key legal and business shifts.
- The limitations of traditional diversity best practices.
- The role of organizational culture in reinforcing inequities.

- The Equity, Cultural Diversity, and Inclusion approach for cultural transformation.
- Strategies for overcoming resistance, engaging leadership, and sustaining DEI efforts.
- Case studies, legal insights, and action plans for implementation.

At the core of this discussion is the need to move beyond performative DEI efforts and embrace strategic, legally sound, and impactful organizational change. Through real-world applications, this book provides cultural diversity practitioners, HR professionals, legal experts, executives, and policymakers with the tools to build resilient, equitable workplaces that withstand legal scrutiny and foster long-term success.

Chapter 1, titled "Diversity, Equity, and Inclusion in Organizations," delves into the definitions and importance of DEI, emphasizing the need for equitable versus equal access to opportunities and resources while fostering engagement and mobility for all individuals. Chapter 2, "The Complex DEI Moral and Legal Landscape," explores the intricate legal and moral challenges associated with DEI efforts, highlighting key legal cases and the struggle to sustain DEI initiatives amidst uncertain and polarized times. Chapter 3, "The Diversity Best Practice Dilemma," discusses the limitations of traditional diversity best practices, emphasizing that implementing these practices alone is insufficient for driving organizational culture change.

Chapter 4, "Social Stratification & Organizational Change," examines how hierarchical relationships and historical governance structures have perpetuated inequities, emphasizing the need for strategic organizational change to address these systemic barriers. Chapter 5, "Organizational Culture & Change," focuses on the role of organizational culture in shaping dynamics and effectiveness, highlighting the need for deliberate shifts in culture to foster inclusivity and equity.

Chapter 6, "Building an Equitable, Culturally Diverse, and Inclusive Organization," introduces the Equity, Cultural Diversity, & Inclusion (ECDI) approach, which provides a comprehensive approach to transforming organizational culture through data-driven strategies. Chapter 7, "Building a Culture of Equity Through Strategic Organizational Change," emphasizes the strategic necessity of embedding equity into organizational culture and outlines a framework for achieving this transformation.

Chapter 8, "An Equity, Cultural Diversity and Inclusion Competency Organizational Culture Change Approach," provides a detailed guide for strategic and continuous planning that align with organizational goals and integrates equity principles into the mission, vision, and operations. Chapter 9, "Create an ECDI Organizational Change Strategic Plan," offers practical advice on engaging leadership, monitoring progress, and sustaining cultural change efforts.

Chapter 10, "Implementation: Navigating the Transformative Journey," explores developing equity and inclusion competency, emphasizing the importance of strategic action and continuous learning to create a sustainable culture of equity. The book concludes with a call to action for DEI practitioners and leaders to embrace these principles and drive meaningful change within their organizations. Finally, Chapter 11, "Mastering Inclusion Competency in the Workplace", explores key ECDI approaches to recruitment, legal compliance, and allyship, offering practical insights from real-world applications rather than purely theoretical ones.

As you engage with this book, I encourage you to challenge assumptions, critically evaluate DEI strategies, and apply the equity-centered approach to drive lasting transformation. DEI is not just about policies. It is about reshaping workplace culture to make equity and inclusion enduring realities so that organizations can better achieve their vision, mission, and talent management strategies.

Chapter 1: Diversity, Equity, and Inclusion in Organizations

DEI, sometimes labeled EDI, refers to actions aimed at creating organizations that are inclusive, equitable, and diverse, valuing cultural differences, ensuring fair access to opportunities and resources, and fostering a sense of engagement and mobility for all individuals. The "D" in DEI represents diversity. This broad term describes the presence and representation of differences within an organization or community, such as race, gender, age, sexual orientation, religion, and physical abilities. This book uses the term "cultural differences" to emphasize and reflect the influence of culture on how people think and behave, as well as the organization's role in shaping behavior. While some DEI best practices have been measured and are evidence-based, their impact on organizational change has not received the attention needed to safeguard against viewing them as distinct from affirmative action. That has made it easier to attack its efficacy.

Equity means ensuring each employee experiences fairness and impartiality in opportunities, treatment, and resource access while considering individual contributors' unique circumstances and needs. Inclusion occurs when everyone in the organization feels a sense of safety, mobility, and reciprocal commitment within an organization. A DEI initiative or program represents a structured solution that organizations implement to integrate diversity, equity, and inclusion into their policies, practices, and culture. Full integration necessarily results in organizational change.

Ideally, a DEI initiative aims to identify and remove systemic barriers and promote fair treatment and representation for all individuals by transforming the organization's culture to serve everyone equitably rather than favoring the interests of specific groups. DEI programs often encompass an initiative or a set of diversity, equity, and inclusion best practices (DEI BPs), such as unconscious bias training, employee resource groups (ERGs), and diversity recruitment, to broadly impact the organization. The goals are to increase workforce diversity, enhance equal opportunity, and cultivate an inclusive environment that retains talent and fosters innovation. It is common to launch a DEI initiative to boost the representation of women and individuals, such as BIPOCs, in leadership roles while ensuring equitable hiring processes and providing mentorship programs.

The cluster of well-established programs and practices promoting diversity and inclusion is called diversity best practices (DEI BP). DEI BP encompasses the techniques, solutions, and actions organizations implement to foster a fair, equitable, and inclusive workplace—ideally supported by research and outcomes. For example, a study published in the International Journal of Advanced Research in Business Management found that blind recruitment, such as the use of resume reviews without the applicant's name or gender, eliminates conscious and unconscious bias, thus increasing cultural diversity in the organization (R. Vivek, 2022). DEI as a profession comprises individuals and teams committed to leading, managing, and implementing DEI and strategies. When effectively executed, implementing DEI BPs, guided by the expertise of DEI practitioners, begins the process of driving transformative change. Yet, DEI BPs are insufficient without embedding in an organizational change strategy. The reputation of implementing DEI BPs as an effective organizational change strategy is largely due to its impressive impact on an organization's success. That success also exposes the weaknesses of DEI BPs for sustaining organizational change, such as the current backlash.

DEI BPs, initiatives, and programs are vital yet distinct solutions for fostering inclusion and equity. Unfortunately, these terms are often used interchangeably, leading to confusion about their specific purposes.

- DEI initiatives refer to targeted projects or actions to achieve specific DEI goals and objectives.

- DEI programs are structured, ongoing efforts designed to embed DEI principles into an organization's culture and operations.
- DEI BPs are proven or well-established methods for addressing challenges such as unconscious bias or poor diversity hiring outcomes.

Despite their unique contributions, these approaches are often misunderstood as interchangeable. This misconception can lead organizations to mistakenly believe that successfully implementing one or more of them marks the end of their DEI journey. In reality, achieving true cultural transformation requires systemic, continuous efforts beyond isolated actions or practices. Any solution not grounded in organizational change methodology is more likely to lead to poor results and expose the organization to backlash.

The confusion between these approaches is further exacerbated by their frequent use as quick fixes. Among them, the DEI BP approach is the most widely adopted. Even the research linking these practices to positive outcomes, such as increased profitability and innovation, has faced scrutiny. Critics argue that the results often lack a direct causal relationship. An article in Personnel Today reported that academics have questioned the robustness of McKinsey's studies demonstrating that DEI impacts the bottom line. They claim that the link between successfully increasing "ethnic" diversity in leadership and financial performance may not be as strong as suggested (Weber, A., 2024, April 12). This shortcoming underscores challenges in achieving broader acceptance and highlights the need for further research to establish how DEI efforts actually drive organizational success.

Research results establishing a causal relationship are more promising when the solutions are incorporated in an organizational change methodology. More organizations truly committed to change using organizational change methodology are needed. The few organizations incorporating DEI into their daily operations, mission, and values—like Microsoft, Deloitte, PwC, and Thomson Reuters—are the exception rather than the rule. Most organizations depend on best practices, initiatives, or programs without fully embracing a comprehensive change framework. This fragmented approach limits DEI's potential and makes it more susceptible to legal and reputational challenges. Cultural diversity is a product of the demographic shift and cannot lead to organizational success without talent management. Only a culture of equity and inclusion can harness cultural diversity in the service of organizational success.

The DEI Return on Investment: The Business Imperative

The impressive, though methodologically questionable, McKinsey research findings are supported by the positive business bottom-line impact observed in companies with successful diversity management culture change approaches. An activist group sent Costco and other major companies a demand letter urging them to review their DEI-related policies and activities and report the return on investment to shareholders. While Costco's board was not obligated to respond to the letter, they responsibly sought shareholder input by polling their views. About 98% of Costco's stockholders voted to sustain the company's DEI efforts. Shareholders are about their bottom line. They do not vote against their investment interests. It is safe to say that they did not vote from a moral or social justice perspective. They did so because they understood that it contributed to the company's success.

The implementation of DEI is often motivated by a moral, brand identity or legal imperative, as in the case of George Floyd's homicide. A CEO may feel compelled to support social justice after a racial disparity incident gains national attention. Others may see DEI as a means to enhance the organization's legal protection or improve brand recognition. Beyond these motivations, DEI has proven to be a strategic business decision that delivers measurable benefits across various aspects of organizational performance (McKinsey, 2020).

DEI enhances the employee experience, fostering fairness, inclusion, and a sense of belonging that drives engagement, productivity, and loyalty. Culturally diverse organizations report higher job performance, fewer sick days, and lower turnover rates. These benefits contribute to the organization's overall agility and resilience in dynamic markets. Furthermore, companies known for their DEI efforts attract top talent, as job seekers increasingly prioritize inclusive work environments. Representation at all levels, particularly in executive roles, strengthens retention, especially among the historically marginalized and excluded members. The talent management advantage DEI offers enhances organizational capacity and innovation.

Organizations with established DEI programs consistently outperform their less committed competitors in key performance areas, including profitability, innovation, and teamwork. Work teams in DEI-committed organizations demonstrate stronger collaboration, agility, and responsiveness to change. These traits are vital in today's competitive business environment. Diversity among the leadership offers a variety of perspectives that drive better decision-making, resulting in sustained financial growth (Smith, J., & Johnson, L., 2016). Moreover, inclusive work environments promote creativity, enabling companies to develop innovative products and services that resonate with a broad customer base. Research underscores these advantages, with studies showing that companies with cultural diversity on executive teams achieve significantly higher profitability (McKinsey & Company, 2020). Unsurprisingly, some attack the soundness of the research associated with these robust findings, which will be discussed later.

Businesses have turned to DEI because the increasingly diverse workforce demands it. Nearly half of all workers are women, and many hold professional roles. BIPOC, nonbinary, and Latinx individuals, among other historically marginalized and excluded group members, make up a growing share of the labor force. Companies that prioritize DEI report higher employee engagement, enhanced market competitiveness, and significant financial gains. The benefits of DEI extend beyond compliance or social responsibility. It positions organizations as industry leaders prepared to thrive in a diverse and ever-changing marketplace. By investing in DEI and committing to systemic cultural transformation, organizations can achieve lasting success while contributing to a more equitable and inclusive society. The early efforts to promote DEI did not have robust research findings to justify the need.

The Evolving DEI Landscape

DEI as a workforce solution has evolved considerably, as covered in my article, "The History of the Diversity Profession and Its Pioneers" (Vaughn, B. E., 2007). The call for companies to value and take direct action to promote a culturally diverse workforce dates back to the 1950s. One of the earliest and most influential reports in this regard was "The Negro and the American Businessman," published in 1954 by President Eisenhower's Committee on Government Contracts. In pursuing a fair, equitable, and engaged workplace, President John F. Kennedy signed Executive Order 10925 in 1961, which required government contractors to "take affirmative action" to ensure that hiring practices were free of racial bias. It was a crucial starting point that spread affirmative action practices beyond the federal government into the private sector, educational institutions, and state and local governments.

President Kennedy's Executive Order 10925 created the foundation for affirmative action and Equal Employment Opportunity. It mandated that government contractors "take affirmative action to ensure that applicants are employed and that employees are treated fairly during employment without regard to their race, creed, color, or national origin." The executive order signaled a shift in the national mindset about diversity in the workplace by formally recognizing the importance of addressing systemic discrimination and promoting fairness in employment practices. Affirmative action, as a result, moved beyond federal contracting mandates, influencing broader societal norms, policies, and practices in education, private business, and government, thus paving the way for subsequent measures, including the Civil Rights Act of 1964 and Executive Order 11246, which expanded affirmative action requirements.

The 1987 report *Workforce 2000: Work and Workers for the Twenty-First Century*, commissioned by the U.S. Department of Labor and prepared by the Hudson Institute with corporate input, was a groundbreaking document that made the business case for workplace diversity (Johnston, W. B., & Packer, A. H., 1987). It analyzed U.S. workforce demographic shifts and projected that by 2000, women, immigrants, and BIPOC individuals would represent a significant portion of the labor force. The report urged businesses to adapt to these changes to remain competitive, prevent discrimination, and address legal risks. It emphasized the moral and economic necessity of recruiting across all population segments, particularly ensuring equitable opportunities for Black Americans. The report also highlighted five critical economic challenges, including (1) fostering global growth, (2) improving service sector productivity, (3) addressing women's workforce needs, (4) integrating diverse groups, and (5) enhancing workers' education and skills.

Workforce 2000 shifted the rationale for diversity from primarily a moral obligation to include a business imperative by linking DEI efforts to talent management. It raised awareness about diversity and inclusion in the workplace but also sparked debates about reverse discrimination and the role of businesses in addressing social issues. The report's influence marked the beginning of diversity in the workplace, especially racial and gender diversity, as a central issue in workplace culture, foreshadowing the cultural battles that would emerge around inclusion efforts. Shortly after, a McKinsey report delved into the challenges organizations would face in attracting and retaining top talent and offered strategic insights to navigate the competitive talent landscape (Chambers, E. G., Foulon, M., Handfield-Jones, H., Hankin, S. M., & Michaels III, E. G., 1998).

Culture Wars

The Workforce 2000 report was pivotal in sparking national conversations about the future of work and the importance of diversity and inclusion. Its conclusions and recommendations raised several concerns that remain today. Some were concerned that its emphasis on increased diversity would lead to divisive policies that favored historically marginalized and excluded groups and, thus, reinforce affirmative action that had grown contentious. Others argued that merit-based talent decisions must remain regardless of societal cultural diversity shifts. Business groups grew concerned about the costs of promoting cultural diversity and the challenges in implementing the initiatives. Academics and policymakers were concerned about the lack of clarity in the report about how to prepare for the demographic shift. Then there was the main street pushback. Historically, the majority and included groups, or White Americans of European ancestry, raised concerns about how their interests would be protected in increased job competition. Even though the reality of the demographic shift and ensuing challenges came to fruition, these concerns are the basis of the current DEI culture wars.

Implementing DEI in today's atmosphere is a complex and often contentious endeavor. Organizations operate in a climate shaped by the ongoing "culture wars" that polarize opinions about DEI's effectiveness and methods for implementing DEI. While DEI's moral and strategic imperatives are well-documented, the field continues to face significant resistance fueled by opposing assumptions about fairness, equality, and equity—terms that can no longer be used interchangeably, as will be discussed. The demographic transformation of the workforce underscores the urgency of DEI efforts. The shifts demand organizational readiness, yet many institutions are hindered by poor cultural diversity management solutions to address the onslaught.

At the same time, DEI practitioners face contradictory expectations and competing assumptions about their work. While it is widely acknowledged that longstanding societal inequities, such as BIPOCs and women's limited access to equal opportunities, have negatively impacted the well-being of historically marginalized and excluded groups, opinions differ on the best approach to address these issues. Some advocate for achieving equality, emphasizing representation, while others prioritize equity, aiming to change the culture that sustains structural barriers. Practices such as diversity recruitment quotas, employee resource groups, and mentorship programs aim to level the playing field. Still, they often stop short of addressing the more deep-rooted inequities embedded in institutional structures. Regardless, the use of practices based on equality assumptions about fairness, though well-intentioned and important, has made it far too easy for opponents of DEI to argue that such measures undermine principles of individual merit and free-market competition.

The opposition has intensified, framing DEI as a challenge to established norms and a violation of the Fourteenth Amendment by discriminating against historically majority and included groups. Anti-DEI activists capitalize on perceived weaknesses, such as an excessive reliance on quotas that may result in hiring less qualified candidates. Furthermore, when implementing DEI is viewed as a charitable endeavor rather than a strategic imperative, such as to morally support Black Lives Matter protests, the programs and initiatives become vulnerable to budget cuts and marginalization, especially during economic downturns. The culture wars surrounding DEI amplify these difficulties, creating an environment where advancing inclusion and equity has become a battleground.

Organizational leaders and DEI practitioners must balance competing forces while fostering collaborative relationships with key stakeholders, addressing structural inequities, and aligning their initiatives with broader organizational objectives. Success in this challenging environment demands a strategy that ensures no one in the organization is left behind and a clear understanding of how societal changes intersect with organizational priorities. The ongoing commitment to fairness begins with a deeper understanding of what fairness means in practice.

Equality Is Not the Same as Equity

We typically ask participants in our managing for racial equity training to define the term equity. Most of them refer to treating people equally and fairly. We explain that equality and equity often need clarification because both refer to treating people fairly. Most participants do not know that there is a difference between the terms. Equality in organizations means treating people the same in terms of opportunities, resources, and support to promote fairness. This assumes that when everyone starts equally, they can successfully compete. The assumption is that the most qualified will naturally rise to the top. Equality is providing the opportunity to each person. In contrast, equity involves giving everyone a fair chance to succeed by providing them with equal resources and opportunities and addressing individual differences in preparation needed to take advantage of equal opportunity. This approach accounts for historical inequities and the additional challenges they create for BIPOCs, ensuring everyone has the support necessary to succeed.

The 400-meter race is a useful scenario for explaining the difference between equity and equality. At first glance, all runners appear to be competing under the same conditions. Each sprinter must run the same distance in a single lap around the track as quickly as possible. If all runners were to begin at the same starting line with starting blocks adjacent to each other, this would represent the equality principle.

Having them start next to each other suggests an equal opportunity. However, we can see that the track curves outward, which means that runners in the outer lanes have a longer distance than those in the inner lanes if no adjustments were made. This would be unfair, despite the appearance of equal treatment.

To correct this imbalance, track officials use staggered starting blocks. This ensures that each runner, regardless of their lane, runs exactly 400 meters. It also means that each adjustment is measured with absolute precision in races that involve curves, such as the 400m race. The staggered start corrects for the structural design of the track that would otherwise create unequal conditions. In this way, the staggered start represents equity, adjusting for differences in position or circumstance so that each athlete has a truly fair chance to succeed. Therefore, equality treats everyone the same regardless of their starting conditions, while equity acknowledges that different people face different challenges, which requires considering ways to level the playing field. As in a 400-meter race, achieving true fairness often requires thoughtful adjustment, not because some people are less capable, but because the systems and structures they operate within are not always fair.

Staggering the starting blocks considers factors like lane width and the curvature of the track, which can impact the distance runners need to cover. The goal is to ensure that all athletes have a fair chance to compete and that the race is decided by skill and effort rather than external factors, such as positioning.

An equity perspective recognizes that providing varying types of support and resources to individuals based on their unique needs and historical backgrounds is necessary to achieve true fairness. As has been pointed out among disability inclusion for a long time, an equity approach to fairness assumes that factors beyond the individual's control, such as past and lingering discrimination, oppression, and injustice, create additional obstacles for some more than others in their efforts to take advantage of equal opportunities. These obstacles have not been welcomed nor are they due to any fault of the individual. Access to quality education, housing discrimination, health disparities, and other inequities make it difficult to level the playing field with equal opportunities alone. Systemic inequities must also be considered and adjusted to create opportunities for people in a diverse society to experience complete fair treatment. The following is a more detailed explanation of the differences.

Equality versus Equity-Oriented DEI

Equality-oriented DEI focuses on treating everyone fairly and ensuring equal representation across people of different cultures. It assumes that some talented individuals have yet to demonstrate their talents due to institutionalized equity barriers, making it imperative to provide them with opportunities. The objective is to eliminate existing biases and institutionalized discrimination by offering equal opportunities and access to resources for all individuals, regardless of their backgrounds or characteristics. Diversity recruitment exemplifies this approach. It emphasizes fairness by treating everyone identically while overlooking historically marginalized and excluded groups' and individuals' unique challenges and disadvantages. The equality assumptions have produced winners and losers along cultural diversity lines in hiring, retention, and promotion decisions.

Equity-oriented DEI, on the other hand, recognizes that the history of workforce exclusion and institutionalized marginalization has resulted in winners and losers at the starting gate, along with biases about how talent is defined and assessed in an increasingly culturally diverse world. The vestiges of institutionalized legal inequity practices that maintain privilege and access for historically majority and included groups continue to impact workplace human resource management and leadership practices today. Despite equal employment opportunity laws, there remains a cultural lag between long-standing inequitable practices and efforts to attract and recruit the best talent. The result is maintaining and reproducing the unfair outcomes that the efforts were meant to address.

To understand the impact of these historical practices, it is essential to consider the context in which they emerged. Human resource management sought to introduce new labor laws in ways that least disrupt an organization's productivity. Many organizations were built on systems that favored certain cultural groups over others before civil rights legislation was passed. The unfortunate result is a lingering legacy of inequality that persists today.

According to McKinsey's research, Black employees in the United States are disproportionately represented in lower-level frontline roles and face significant barriers in advancing up the corporate ladder. They are promoted from entry-level at lower rates than their organization's representation. This phenomenon is often called the "broken rung" in the corporate ladder. Coupled with higher attrition rates among Black employees, the barriers to upward mobility create a shortage of Black leaders in many institutions, preventing these organizations from fully benefiting from the advantages of cultural diversity. Even those Black employees who successfully attain managerial positions rarely advance to the highest levels of leadership within their organizations.

Black employees are also disproportionately hired for low-wage, physically demanding, and dangerous jobs as a result of these systemic issues. Here are a few examples:

1. Service Industry: Black Americans work in various roles, such as food service workers, janitors, custodians, and housekeepers. These jobs often involve low wages that can be physically demanding and too often dangerous. Unfortunately, they are sometimes associated with higher levels of risk, including exposure to hazardous chemicals or potential workplace accidents.

2. Transportation and Delivery: Black Americans are employed as truck, delivery, and bus drivers, or taxi drivers in the transportation

sector. These jobs tend to be physically and mentally demanding and involve long hours, increasing the risk of accidents and fatigue-related incidents.

3. Construction: Black Americans also work in the construction industry, where they are employed as laborers, carpenters, or masons. Construction work is physically demanding and potentially hazardous, with physical risks such as falls, exposure to harmful substances, and heavy machinery accidents.

4. Healthcare Support: In the healthcare industry, Black Americans may be more likely to work in support roles, such as nursing assistants, medical aides, or patient transporters. These positions often involve low wages and can be physically demanding, as they require lifting and assisting patients, working in high-stress environments, and potentially being exposed to infectious diseases.

5. Retail and Customer Service: Black Americans may also work in the retail sector as cashiers, sales associates, or customer service representatives. These jobs can involve long hours, low wages, and dealing with demanding customers, all of which can contribute to a stressful work environment.

It is essential to recognize that the representation of Black Americans in these jobs is not due to their qualifications or abilities but rather a result of systemic inequities, discrimination, and limited access to different opportunities. Efforts to address these disparities and create more equitable workplaces require carefully assessing barriers to equity and removing them to increase equity.

Low-wage, harmful job roles are ongoing realities that are all too familiar to BIPOC employees, as indicated by the stories shared about inequities with their Black friends, family members, and colleagues, communication that reinforces their collective disparate workplace experiences. These stories also follow them psychologically from one workplace to the next. It only takes a single incident to reinforce existing assumptions about racism. It can be a verbal slight, off-color remark, or pay inequity to alert them to behaviors that express unfairness. These stories are also shared in assessment interviews.

In summary, racial equality is about treating people fairly, while racial equity is about creating fair and just systems and conditions that produce the opportunity for equal outcomes. Creating fairness that drives talent requires ensuring Historically marginalized and excluded groups receive what they need to thrive. Let us look more closely at managing equity in the workplace, which is key to treating people fairly based on their unique circumstances and needs. In the next section, we delve into how the cultural and political debates surrounding DEI create obstacles for advancing equity. We explore the assumptions fueling these divisions and their implications for organizations and practitioners.

What is Resistance to DEI?

Resistance to DEI significantly hinders progress toward creating equitable and inclusive workplaces. It arises from various root causes and manifests in forms ranging from skepticism to outright hostility. Addressing this resistance requires understanding its origins, which include perceived threats to norms, ignorance of DEI's purpose, political polarization, and fear of change. DEI efforts often challenge assumptions about fairness and longstanding organizational practices, prompting some to view them as threats to established norms, traditions, or hierarchies. Changing policies for hiring, promotion, or workplace practices are perceived as undermining meritocracy and free-market principles, sparking backlash from those who feel that they are being displaced or disadvantaged. Many opponents of DEI view it as a mechanism for redressing historical grievances rather than adding value to the organization and workforce.

Political polarization is also critical, with DEI caught in broader culture wars. Opponents often dismiss DEI as social engineering, arguing that it undermines meritocracy, individual freedoms, and "colorblind" principles. Many reject DEI's ethical imperative to address systemic inequities, asserting that they bear no responsibility for historical injustices, thus oppose measures they see as prioritizing quotas or unfair advantages for historically marginalized and historical group members.

Fear of change and anticipated loss of privilege also drive resistance. DEI initiatives may evoke fears of losing power, influence, or status among those benefiting from existing systems. Political fear tactics amplify this resistance, especially among influential individuals reluctant to accept evidence of DEI's benefits or threatened by its success. Poor education about DEI's goals, historical institutionalized barriers to equity, and misalignment with organizational objectives exacerbate misunderstandings. Additionally, poorly implemented DEI initiatives, often due to insufficient training or institutional support, can reinforce skepticism by appearing ineffective or misaligned with business needs.

To overcome resistance, organizations must address assumptions about fairness, highlight DEI's value to the workforce, and ensure initiatives are carefully designed, well-supported, and aligned with organizational goals. Understanding the forms of resistance and their impact is crucial for creating a plan for reducing them.

Forms of Resistance

A 2023 Pew Research Center survey found that while 56% of American workers support advancing diversity in the workplace and implementing DEI, only 32% consider workplace diversity a personal priority. This reflects a phenomenon I label "ambivalent inclusion", where individuals outwardly support inclusion but unconsciously hold biases rooted in hierarchical views of race, gender, and merit. For example, a manager advocating for diverse hiring may hesitate to promote a qualified African American woman vying for upward mobility due to ingrained prejudices about talent, offering placations rather than advancement. Similarly, pay disparities, such as women earning less than equally qualified male colleagues in the same job role, often go unnoticed until scrutinized by HR or challenged legally. Structural barriers like siloed hierarchies, lack of leadership commitment, and insufficient resources represent other forms of resistance that undermine DEI efforts.

A history of inconsistent institutional support for historically marginalized group professionals and ongoing systemic inequities has fueled skepticism about organizations' genuine commitment to DEI. As a result, existing hierarchies often remain intact, perpetuating unfairness instead of driving systemic change. The workplace equity movement seeks to dismantle these barriers and increase decision-makers' awareness and understanding of the negative impact of passive or ambivalent actions. Performative actions, such as celebrating cultural holidays or appointing DEI leaders without real authority, expertise or resources, further limit impact and erode trust. Resistance also appears through direct opposition, including lobbying against inclusion policies, filing reverse discrimination or hostile workplace lawsuits, and framing DEI programs as discriminatory. Public grieving on social media, especially in response to racially charged events or policies like transgender restroom access, intensifies resistance and creates politically charged environments that obstruct DEI progress. Understanding and addressing this resistance is critical to embedding DEI as a sustainable, transformative force within organizational culture.

Chapter 2: The Complex DEI Moral and Legal Landscape

Economic uncertainty, political backlash, and legal challenges have prompted many organizational leaders to reduce or abandon their DEI initiatives. They primarily represent those with a history of cautious commitment due to legal risk aversion and leadership bias towards the initiatives. The recent retreat has highlighted how leaders struggle to balance legal risk protection and anti-DEI activism while aiming to preserve the competitive advantages and long-term benefits of DEI programs. Compounding this complexity is the overt and covert resistance evidenced by legal disputes, public criticism, and internal opposition from employees and stakeholders. Employees who prioritize DEI in their workplace, particularly younger generation workers, urge their organizations to enhance commitment to DEI principles.

CEOs are managing demands from external activist organizations to bolster or diminish their DEI policies (Keena, A., 2025, March 8). This dual force of resistance and advocacy highlights the broader societal polarization that increasingly shapes workplace dynamics. It underscores the urgency for organizations to develop strategies for building consensus among employees and other stakeholders while mitigating legal risk. Navigating competing perspectives, shifting priorities, and deep social, political, and legal divides driven by demographic changes is part of the DEI practitioner's work. The challenge is not insurmountable.

This chapter explores the multifaceted challenges organizations face when engaging in DEI work, mainly how it has been framed as contradictory to meritocracy and legally unlawful. Critics often argue that DEI initiatives compromise fairness by emphasizing group identity over individual merit. However, they frequently fail to account for well-acknowledged systemic inequities and entrenched societal barriers perpetuating disparities in opportunity and access. The discussion highlights the uneven levels of commitment among organizational leaders, with some championing DEI as a core value and others retreating under pressure, viewing it as both a vital business commitment and a contentious and risky undertaking that leaders must confront straightforwardly.

Generally, this chapter examines the opportunities and obstacles of advancing DEI during an era of heightened divisiveness and uncertainty. It offers leaders and practitioners valuable insights into the forces shaping the DEI discourse. Beyond fulfilling legal and ethical responsibilities, embracing DEI fosters innovation, creativity, and resilience, giving organizations a competitive advantage in an increasingly diverse and interconnected world. The complexity of the legal landscape, the struggle to sustain DEI during uncertainty, the opposing views about the utility of DEI, and how a creative coexistence philosophy can reduce turbulence are discussed.

The Legal Landscape and Key Cases

Is DEI a liability or an essential commitment for organizations? Let's consider Google's efforts to implement DEI to safeguard against legal risks. The company appointed its first Head of Diversity in 2005, marking the beginning of formal DEI initiatives. In 2013, unconscious bias training programs were implemented to help employees recognize and mitigate unintended prejudices. The company set a goal in 2020 to increase leadership roles held by underrepresented groups by 30% by 2025. However, in February 2025, Google announced it would no longer set diversity hiring targets and is reviewing its DEI programs.

In the meantime, three female former employees filed a 2017 class-action lawsuit against Google, alleging that the company systematically underpaid women and assigned them to lower job levels compared to their male counterparts, violating California's Equal Pay Act. The plaintiffs claimed these practices led to disparities in pay and career advancement opportunities for women at Google. In June 2022, Google agreed to a $118 million settlement to resolve these allegations, covering approximately 15,500 female employees in California employed since September 14, 2013.

In March 2025, Google agreed to a $28 million settlement in response to a class-action lawsuit alleging that the company favored white and Asian employees over other racial groups. The lawsuit, led by former employee Ana Cantu, who identifies as Mexican and racially Indigenous, claimed that these employees received higher pay and were placed on more advantageous career tracks, thereby disadvantaging Hispanic, Latinx, Indigenous, Native American, Native Hawaiian, Pacific Islander, and Alaska Native employees. The settlement covers at least 6,632 employees in California employed between February 15, 2018, and December 31, 2024.

In each case, Google was sued for ongoing, illegal, and systematic discrimination against historically marginalized and excluded groups. In both instances, Google agreed to substantial financial settlements without admitting wrongdoing, aiming to resolve the disputes and potentially avoid prolonged litigation. In February 2025, and just before the most recent settlement, Google announced it would no longer set diversity hiring targets and is reviewing its DEI programs. This is an example of how an organization views and treats DEI primarily from a legal perspective and how the risk of lawsuits is not guaranteed when the initiative or programs are not legally sound or fail to address systemic inequities.

Implementing DEI is imperative for modern organizations. Yet, it has always been closely linked to reducing risk. Companies began implementing workforce diversity training as a legal safeguard following the passage of the Civil Rights Act of 1964, particularly Title VII, which prohibits workplace discrimination based on race, color, religion, sex, or national origin. This landmark legislation, coupled with the expansion of anti-discrimination laws, heightened societal expectations for making progress, and the growing threat of litigation created significant legal obligations for employers. Providing diversity training to an organization's entire workforce was necessary to demonstrate compliance with the law and reduce liability (Vaughn, B. E., 2007).

In the 1970s and 1980s, affirmative action policies further accelerated the adoption of workplace diversity programs. These policies aimed to promote the hiring and advancement of historically marginalized and excluded groups, prompting companies to use training programs to address employee resistance and foster cultural awareness. Over time, diversity training evolved to promote inclusion and as a strategic tool for mitigating legal and organizational risks associated with non-compliance.

The 1990s marked a turning point, with workplace harassment lawsuits highlighting the need for proactive measures. High-profile cases, such as those involving sexual harassment allegations, brought attention to organizational vulnerabilities. A Supreme Court 1998 ruling in Faragher v. City of Boca Raton and Burlington Industries, Inc. v. Ellerth underscored that companies could be held liable for harassment unless they could prove they had implemented reasonable preventative measures, including training programs (Faragher v. City of Boca Raton, 524 U.S. 775., 1998). These decisions cemented diversity training as a standard corporate practice for mitigating liability.

In the 2000s, class-action lawsuits, including Dukes v. Walmart Stores, Inc., which tackled gender discrimination, highlighted systemic inequities in hiring and promotion practices. In response, companies increasingly embraced diversity training to showcase their commitment to fostering equity and inclusion. These programs also played a crucial role in protecting companies' reputations as public expectations for fair workplaces grew. Today, diversity training has become a standard compliance resource. While legal regulatory bodies like the Equal Employment Opportunity Commission (EEOC) have traditionally advocated for training to address workplace discrimination and harassment proactively, the federal government's attempts to dismantle those entities are underway under the current leadership. Companies with five or more employees in California must provide mandatory sexual harassment training every two years. Training programs also cover more nuanced issues, such as implicit bias and microaggressions, to establish a record of an organization's commitment to preventing workplace inequalities.

By integrating diversity training into their DEI strategies, companies reduce the risk of lawsuits and position themselves as socially responsible entities to potential employees and customers. Some critics argue that implementing DEI to prioritize legal protection does not lead to changes in the culture impacting inclusion and equity, leading to ineffective outcomes, workplace resistance, and a temporary legal band-aid. Others generally believe diversity training contributes to a hostile workplace due to a presumed emphasis on targeting White historically majority people as oppressors and the privileged. Despite these challenges, diversity training has remained a cornerstone of modern DEI practices, balancing compliance needs with efforts to build more inclusive workplace environments. This dual purpose of risk mitigation and culture-building has solidified its role in corporate risk management strategies. The path forward is creating cultures that do not exclude anyone while addressing culturally diverse needs.

It is logical to conclude that the workforce must navigate cultural differences for operational success and legal protection against unlawful behaviors and their consequences. Employees must collaborate productively, including treating one another with civility and professionalism. This does not happen simply because employees believe and state that they are open and tolerant. Even when a person treats others as they would like to be treated, cultural differences often influence how individuals prefer to be treated to achieve successful interactions. This is why cultural diversity is used in this book instead of the term diversity alone. Cultural differences emphasize differences due to sharing a unique worldview that impacts the way people define themselves, how they get things done, power dynamics, etc. This is a primary reason for misunderstandings in the DEI initiative occurring in design and delivery.

Over the years, several high-profile lawsuits have highlighted the challenges and legal complexities surrounding implementing DEI:

- De Piero v. Pennsylvania State University: Zack K. De Piero, an historically majority and included group English composition professor, filed a lawsuit alleging a hostile work environment due to the university's DEI implementation. He claimed that the training and discussions used racial stereotypes and claims that suggest a person's success, behavior, or potential is pre-determined by their race, creating a racially hostile work environment for them. The court allowed his racial harassment legal claim to proceed, emphasizing that the alleged discrimination was frequent and unavoidable, though his First Amendment retaliation and other claims were dismissed.

- Diemert v. City of Seattle: Joshua Diemert, a former program intake representative, alleged that the City of Seattle's Race and Social Justice Initiative (RSJI) created a racially hostile work environment. He faced harassment and retaliation for opposing race-based training that promoted concepts like "white privilege." The court found his claims of a hostile work environment, disparate treatment, and retaliation plausible, allowing them to proceed to trial. The city prevailed on February 10, 2025, when the United States District Court, Western District of Washington, ruled in its favor.

- Students for Fair Admissions v. Harvard: This Supreme Court case challenged Harvard's race-conscious admissions policies, arguing they discriminated against Asian American applicants. The court ruled that Harvard's admissions system violated the Equal Protection Clause, declaring affirmative action in college admissions unconstitutional. This decision has broad implications for race-based DEI practices nationwide. Organizations committed to DEI are scrambling to devise an action to adjust to the legal rulings.

- <u>Young v. Colorado Department of Corrections.</u> The Tenth Circuit Court examined a case involving a former employee of the Department of Corrections. The correction officer claimed that the mandatory diversity training depicted white employees, including himself, as inherently racist, which he found offensive and detrimental to his ability to perform effectively in an already racially charged prison atmosphere. He believed that the training created a hostile and unsafe work environment, resulting in heightened racial tensions among staff and inmates. Although the court ultimately dismissed his claims, it cautioned that DEI programs could indeed foster hostile workplaces if they involve ongoing stereotyping and discriminatory expectations.

The pervasiveness of actions in an organization that constitute hostility is what matters from a legal point of view.

Evidence presented in the De Piero v. Pennsylvania State University lawsuit is a good example. As stated above, the case centered around DEI training and initiatives that Zack De Piero, a professor at Penn State Abington, alleged created a hostile work environment. The detailed allegations include several key components of the training and related activities:

- <u>Conversation on Racial Climate:</u> In June 2020, De Piero was required to attend a session led by the Assistant Vice Provost for Educational Equity, Alina Wong. During this session, Wong conducted a breathing exercise where she singled out white and non-black individuals, asking them to hold their breath longer than others. Wong explained that this was to make them "feel the pain" experienced by George Floyd and caused by systemic racism.

- <u>Comments on Classroom Dynamics</u>: A colleague informed De Piero that resistance to wearing masks to prevent the spread of COVID-19 was more likely to occur in classrooms taught by women and people of color, mainly when historically majority and included group participants voiced resistance.

- <u>Email from DEI Director</u>: De Piero received an email from Aneesah Smith, Director of DEI, which addressed all Penn State employees. In this email, Smith, who identified as a "Queer, Christian, Cisgender woman of color," called on "white" people to confront their internalized white supremacy and to hold other white employees accountable. She instructed "White" individuals to stop talking and to listen instead.

- <u>Black Linguistic Justice</u>: In August 2020, Liliana Naydan, De Piero's department chair, sent an email advocating for "Black Linguistic Justice," urging faculty to ensure that students recognize white supremacy in language and writing pedagogy. Another email from Naydan declared that "reverse racism isn't racism."

- <u>Professional Development Meeting</u>: In October 2020, De Piero attended a mandatory professional development meeting led by Naydan and Assistant Teaching Professor Grace Lee-Amuzie. They provided examples of what they considered racist comments made by professors, exclusively using comments made by White professors.

- <u>Training Video</u>: De Piero received repeated emails from a colleague urging him to watch a training video titled "White Teachers Are a Problem." In the video, race activist Asao Inoue criticized White colleagues as "the problem" and claimed that "White English kills people of color."

- <u>"Arts and Humanities as Activism" Event</u>: In November 2020, De Piero's interim division supervisor was required to attend an event featuring Dr. Aja Martinez. Martinez condemned race neutrality, equal opportunity, color blindness, and merit, calling them tools of "White elites" protecting white supremacy. Naydan endorsed these views in follow-up emails, encouraging their incorporation into departmental teaching.

- Antiracist Pedagogy Meeting: In January 2021, De Piero had to attend another meeting where Naydan endorsed grading students based on race, applying more lenient standards to non-white students.

- Bias Report Mechanism: In the spring of 2021, De Piero reported discrimination and harassment through the university's Bias Report mechanism. In September 2021, when he met with the Associate Director of Penn State Affirmative Action, he was told there was a problem with the white race and advised to continue attending antiracist programming.

- White Historically Majority Group Instructors Address White Privilege in Their Classrooms: In October 2021, De Piero participated in a mandatory training session where Naydan presented content that charged white faculty with perpetuating racist discourses and practices in their classrooms. While it is unclear what the course contents were and how it was facilitated, De Piero appears to have felt that it was demeaning and hostile.

De Piero's experiences highlighted in the court case illustrate the problems created when those responsible for DEI training and initiatives target historically majority and included group individuals based on the assumption that they harbor racism.

The plaintiffs' complaints, whether valid or not, arose when historically majority and included group members of the campus community felt racially stereotyped and harassed. Challenges stemming from the classroom behaviors of some historically majority and included group instructors may have warranted training, but the execution of that remediation training was flawed. None of us likes to be treated as though we are prejudiced, intolerant, and discriminate based on a person's race. Instead of addressing systemic racism and fostering change, their confrontational approach inadvertently perpetuated the racism they aimed to reduce, at least as experienced by De Piero. DEI practitioners risk undermining their work—and the organization's efforts—when any group feels excluded or perceives itself as being attacked. Labels like "white privilege" or "oppressor" can provoke resistance or backlash if their impact on each segment of the audience isn't carefully considered. To prevent this, DEI initiatives must be designed with empathy and grounded in proven, well-tested solutions. This calls for better practitioner training rather than dismantling DEI.

Recent legal challenges complicate the DEI landscape. Consider the Diemert v. City of Seattle and the Students for Fair Admissions v. Harvard University cases. Joshua Diemert first sued the City of Seattle in 2020, claiming that he was subjected to persistent exposure to racial discrimination and harassment resulting from the city's Race and Social Justice Initiative (RSJI). He alleged that the city's mandatory diversity training and programs created a hostile work environment for him as a "white male." Diemert contended that these programs, which focused on addressing systemic racism, were discriminatory and ultimately forced him to resign from his position.

Before the regional court heard the case, the City of Seattle filed a motion for summary judgment, asking the court to dismiss the case without going to trial. In 2024, the regional court ruled in favor of the City of Seattle, granting the motion for summary judgment. The court concluded that Diemert's claims lacked sufficient evidence and that, as a matter of law, the RSJI did not create a hostile work environment or constitute discrimination. The final decision on January 10, 2025, upheld this earlier ruling, affirming that the RSJI program was not inherently discriminatory and that the evidence provided by Diemert was not enough to support his claims.

Another landmark case, Students for Fair Admissions v. Harvard, has redefined affirmative action and race and gender-conscious policies, reshaping the parameters within which DEI efforts are operationalized.

The *Students for Fair Admissions v. Harvard* case was a landmark legal battle that centered on whether Harvard University's admissions practices discriminated against Asian American applicants in violation of federal civil rights laws, specifically Title VI of the Civil Rights Act of 1964, which prohibits racial discrimination by institutions receiving federal funding.

The Students for Fair Admissions (SFFA) lawsuit accused Harvard of using racial preferences in its admissions process that unfairly harmed Asian American applicants. Specifically, Harvard limited the number of Asian Americans admitted to the university despite their higher academic performance compared to other racial groups. SFFA argued that Harvard's use of race as a factor in admissions violated the Equal Protection Clause of the 14th Amendment and Title VI of the Civil Rights Act, prohibiting racial discrimination.

Harvard defended its admissions practices by pointing out that its review process is holistic in that race is merely one of many factors considered in its efforts to achieve its mission of a diverse student body, which it argued was consistent with Supreme Court ruling precedent that allows race-conscious admissions policies under certain conditions. In an October 2018 district court ruling, the U.S. District Court for the District of Massachusetts ruled in favor of Harvard University, dismissing SFFA's claims. The court concluded that Harvard's admissions process did not discriminate against Asian American applicants. The judge wrote in their opinion that Harvard's admissions policy was not motivated by racial animus and that the university's consideration of race as a factor was lawful under the guidelines set by the U.S. Supreme Court in previous cases, such as *Grutter v. Bollinger* (2003). The judge acknowledged that Asian Americans, on average, had lower "personal ratings" (which included subjective assessments like personality traits and likability) in Harvard's admissions process, but ruled that this did not constitute discrimination, and that race was only one factor among many in the admissions decision.

SFFA appealed the decision to the U.S. Court of Appeals for the First Circuit. In November 2020, the First Circuit upheld the lower court's ruling in a 2-1 decision. The appellate court found that Harvard's admissions process complied with Supreme Court precedents regarding the use of race in college admissions and did not amount to racial discrimination. The court reaffirmed that Harvard had a compelling interest in achieving a diverse student body and that its use of race was narrowly tailored, meaning it did not constitute an undue burden on Asian American applicants. The majority opinion emphasized that it was thus legal for Harvard to consider race as a factor to achieve its diversity mission, which it found to be a legitimate educational goal. However, one of the noted concerns was the subjective nature of the "personal rating" and the potential for unconscious bias, but ultimately, the court upheld Harvard's process.

SFFA appealed to the U.S. Supreme Court, requesting the Court review the case. In January 2022, the Supreme Court agreed to hear the case. On June 29, 2023, the U.S. Supreme Court ruled in a 6-3 majority that Harvard University's race-conscious admissions policies violated the Equal Protection Clause of the 14th Amendment. The Court's decision effectively overturned earlier precedents that allowed race to be considered in college admissions. The Court concluded that the use of race in Harvard's admissions process was not narrowly tailored and that the university's efforts to achieve diversity were insufficient to justify the racial preferences. The decision ruled that race-based affirmative action was unconstitutional in the context of college admissions, calling for institutions to pursue race-neutral alternatives.

This ruling marked a significant change in the legal landscape regarding affirmative action and hiring, promotion, and admissions quotas. It was part of a broader trend in which the Court's conservative majority expressed skepticism about race-conscious policies. As a result, it became clear that universities would need to adopt race-neutral approaches in their admissions processes. This case has profoundly impacted higher education's efforts to promote diversity, particularly how universities incorporate diversity and inclusion goals into their admissions processes moving forward. It also emboldened the anti-DEI activists. They have sent letters to businesses claiming that the decision against Harvard was evidence that all types of programs and initiatives that are identity group-based are discriminatory, thus illegal.

These decisions reinforce the importance of aligning DEI initiatives with evolving legal standards while maintaining a steadfast commitment to equity. Despite these challenges, forward-thinking organizations create innovative approaches to pave a pathway forward. For instance, Thomas Jefferson High School for Science and Technology (TJHSST)'s race-neutral admissions policy demonstrates how focusing on socioeconomic cultural diversity and holistic evaluations can promote equity while enduring legal scrutiny.

TJHSST's successful defense of its admissions policy is likely attributed to the administration's commitment to upholding minimum standards for individual merit. In 2020, high school administration significantly transformed its admissions process. Previously, standardized test scores played a prominent role in admissions decisions. The revised process eliminated standardized testing. Instead, it implemented a system that allocated equal slots to students from each middle school in the county based on their GPA. Being in the top tier of graduates at your school offered you the best chance of entrance after the additional achievement test requirement was eliminated.

These changes were intended to foster inclusion and increase cultural diversity within the school without explicitly factoring in race. The new policy also gave more weight to economically disadvantaged applicants or English language learners. One key reason the Supreme Court declined to hear the case challenging the admissions program was its emphasis on individual merit within each feeder school. Applicants who ranked in the top ten percent of their class at each school within the recruitment area were virtually guaranteed admission, provided all other criteria were met. Notably, the policy increased admissions for groups that had been difficult to recruit. The approach also reduced the number of Asian Americans admitted, while maintaining the percentage above their overall population size. Yet, their percentage among the total admitted remained the highest.

The glaring difference is that fairness in the selection decisions at Thomas Jefferson School is based on an equity approach rather than equality or affirmative action, where everyone is required to take an achievement test that is known to produce consistently biased outcomes. The assumption is that if a person succeeds in a school with limited resources, they have demonstrated readiness that an achievement test cannot fully capture. An equity approach acknowledges their success while recognizing other valid ways to evaluate it. TJHSST has enhanced equity in admissions by creating strategies to include the historically excluded without undermining the principles of merit. The lesson for practitioners is that an equality approach maintains the status quo, while an equity approach can transform an organization's culture. These strategies showcase what is needed to achieve DEI goals in today's polarized environment.

White Historically Majority Group Resistance to DEI

Research indicates that many HMIG members become more resistant to supporting DEI after being "put in the hot seat" or confronted about their prejudice or privilege. The negative response to these experiences leads some individuals to conclude that they must be prejudiced. The negative response to the experience has been shown to cause some of them to decide that they must be prejudiced (Devine, P. G., Monteith, M. J., Zuwerink, J. R., & Elliot, A. J., 1991). Others were more open to receiving information countering their open and tolerant self-concept.

They decided more was needed to align their actions with their inclusive values. They sought ways to increase their inclusive competence.

This research inspired me to create a self-confrontation technique that reduce resistance to discussing DEI topics such as unconscious bias, privilege, and meritocracy. The Powerful Questions technique is a non-intimidating method that uses questions to encourage participants to think critically about their values and beliefs regarding a subject. This technique will be discussed in more detail later in this book.

In summary, practitioners' best intentions to help their audience cultivate empathy for and mutual understanding of cultural differences among colleagues in their organization can unexpectedly go off track without carefully considering how to treat everyone equitably and inclusively. Poorly designed and executed DEI practices can increase legal risks, especially when they create a hostile work environment.

Affirmative Action on Trial: Balancing Equity and Merit in a Divided Nation

Affirmative action became a prominent approach to addressing historical injustices and promoting equality in the United States during the mid-20th century. It emerged as a response to systemic racial discrimination, segregation, and exclusion, particularly in education and employment. Affirmative action aimed to create pathways for historically marginalized groups to access opportunities previously denied. It has been pushed at the federal level as an intervention to dismantle segregation and discriminatory practices, leading to landmark legislation like the Civil Rights Act of 1964.

Arguments in favor of affirmative action emphasize addressing historical injustices, promoting equality, and fostering a more diverse and inclusive society and workplace. Opposition to affirmative action, however, has existed since its inception and has increased over time.

Dissenting views reflect concerns about fairness, meritocracy, and reverse discrimination. The opposition has resorted to legal challenges based on the U.S. Constitution's Equal Protection Clause, particularly the idea that all individuals are entitled to equal treatment under the law. The 1868 clause was created to protect the rights of newly freed slaves of African descent following the Civil War, ensuring that all individuals, regardless of race, would be treated equally under the law. Court rulings have reinforced the principle of equal treatment by states unless a strong justification exists. However, the Equal Protection Clause does not apply to private individuals or businesses unless they receive federal funds, work for the government, or operate under state laws mandating affirmative action.

The Equal Protection Clause is often invoked to challenge affirmative action, arguing that favoring certain racial or gender groups violates equal protection principles. The Supreme Court has revisited this contentious issue multiple times, including in landmark cases such as Regents of the University of California v. Bakke (1978), Fisher v. University of Texas (2016), and the more recent Students for Fair Admissions, Inc. v. President and Fellows of Harvard College (2023). These rulings highlight the ongoing tension between fairness, aiming to address lingering inequalities from the past, and upholding meritocracy by treating individuals equally, regardless of their background. While the 1978 Bakke decision allowed the use of race with certain restrictions, the 2023 ruling imposed more stringent limitations, illustrating the evolving legal and societal debate surrounding affirmative action.

Apart from voluntary actions, businesses have largely remained unaffected, while higher education has repeatedly defended its efforts. For decades, the business sector has relied on implementing DEI best practices (DEI BPs) to show a commitment to welcoming different cultures and ethnic groups and to meet recruitment needs in an increasingly culturally diverse job applicant pool. However, the backlash against DEI, particularly those perceived as conflicting with established values of individual merit and self-reliance, has created significant legal and organizational challenges for practitioners and organizational leaders.

The Struggle to Sustain DEI Efforts in Uncertain and Polarized Times

The ongoing challenges surrounding DEI have persisted, fluctuating with shifts in the political climate, legal decisions, and demographic changes. The past and current attacks on DEI in the United States reflect long-standing hostility toward affirmative action, particularly in education and business. As stated, many leaders of organizations that lacked a firm DEI commitment publicly expressed support for social justice in response to the George Floyd protests, feeling pressured to take a stand. They allocated resources to implement DEI initiatives and hire DEI practitioners. Those with existing DEI programs reaffirmed their commitment and contributed to charitable organizations like Black Lives Matter.

A group of wealthy anti-DEI individuals noticed the increased interest in support for DEI. They view DEI as an anti-democratic, divisive tool that undermines "American" values, funded by unsuspecting corporate and institutional leaders. Their voices were amplified during the administration of the forty-fifth president, D. Trump of the United States. Six months after George Floyd lost his life in police custody, a presidential executive order halted DEI efforts in the federal government. The attacks on DEI continued after J. Biden became the 46th American president and took office in 2021. Biden signed an executive order to overturn the previous administration's anti-DEI order, restoring DEI in the federal government workplace (Biden, J. Jr., 2021, June 25). However, after the 2024 elections, the forty-seventh administration shifted again, moving away from DEI and affirmative action, introducing an anti-DEI executive order that strengthened the opposition.

Considerable damage had been done, and DEI became a polarizing term. The attacks on DEI escalated after the Supreme Court struck down Harvard's use of race in admissions decisions. The monied resistance, bolstered by a Supreme Court conservative majority, increased use of legal means to undermine DEI, and recent Supreme Court decisions indicate they have made headway. Those funding the case against Harvard, such as Edward Blum of the Heritage Foundation and the Searle Freedom Trust, are examples

The DEI debate hinges on differing views of fairness. Supporters, including academics, urban educators, and practitioners, see growing diversity and institutional barriers limiting participation in politics, education, and employment, reinforcing systemic advantages for historically majority and included groups. Many DEI proponents call out structural inequities that restrict the ability of immigrants, women, LGBTQIA+ individuals, and other persons to participate in and contribute to society fully. Some advocate for affirmative action policies, such as diversity recruitment quotas, to quickly address these disparities and create a more equitable environment. Both perspectives are based on the view that societal inequities are deeply rooted and difficult to change, yet ultimately harm everyone. They disagree about how serious the problem is and how to address it.

Advocates of DEI maintain that disenfranchising individuals based solely on citizenship status, culture, gender, or race is immoral and undemocratic. They assert that stronger government policies and improved equal rights legislation are crucial for tackling these issues and promoting a fairer and more inclusive society. The opposing view stresses individual rights over group grievances, with a focus on promoting equality to level the playing field so that everyone has an equal chance to succeed without "reverse discrimination." From this perspective, individuals will be better off if they support the free market and allow individuals to compete with minimal government intervention.

While the case centered on harm to Asian American applicants who were perceived as victims of discrimination due to the admissions policy, a wealthy, historically majority and included group conservative male activist led the legal effort under the guise of a student activist organization. The organization claimed to represent the interests of Asian American applicants who felt Harvard's affirmative action policies had unjustly disadvantaged them. Although the organization allegedly represented a coalition of students and parents, no Asian American was a plaintiff. The court's decision led many higher education leaders to curb or withdraw from implementing DEI, with a growing number following suit. In some instances, in-house DEI practitioners, who once reported directly to the organization's leadership, were reassigned under human resources managers and equal opportunity officers, diminishing their authority.

A war is also being waged against DEI content and materials in education, starting with K-12 education. Parents actively working to remove textbooks they believe promote "socialist" ideologies and conflict with their values are typically motivated by a deep concern for preserving what they see as traditional "American" values. These parents, often holding conservative or libertarian views, are particularly opposed to educational content they perceive as promoting progressive social values. They fear such content undermines the ideals of capitalism, individualism, and patriotism, which they regard as core to American identity.

While some parents scrutinize textbook content, particularly in subjects like history, social studies, and literature, where they feel narratives may be tailored to reflect a more progressive or left-leaning perspective, others reject books based solely on the prejudice against a title or author. These groups are active in their local communities and school boards, often organizing or joining coalitions to advocate for removing specific textbooks and adopting materials more aligned with their values. Their activism frequently involves attending school board meetings, removing progressive board members, supporting the election of board members who share their ideology, petitioning, and campaigning for changes to curriculum policies.

Some parents also engage in legal challenges or political campaigns to influence education policy, working with politicians or legal organizations that share their views on educational content. They have successfully recalled school board members whom they felt did not listen to or align with their views. These community activists have achieved local successes in challenging the adoption of textbooks they view as biased, particularly those concerning race, gender, and oppression, which they believe promote a progressive agenda. In certain instances, they have influenced curriculum changes, resulting in the adoption of alternative materials that align with their beliefs. Texts they were assigned in school, such as Maya Angelou's works, are now deemed off-limits for their children. Public campaigns are another method used to raise awareness and garner support for their cause, framing their efforts as a defense of children's education and parental rights. Their actions reflect a broader national debate over the content of public education, underscoring the significant ideological divisions regarding how American history and values should be taught in schools.

Anti-DEI activism expanded into the business sector despite the Harvard admissions case having little direct impact on most companies. Opponents cited concerns over hiring practices, corporate funding of social justice groups, and programs supporting Black women entrepreneurs. DEI practitioners faced heightened scrutiny, especially after Hamas attacked Israeli citizens and took hostages on October 7, 2023, escalating the Israel-Hamas war and intensifying ideological divisions in the U.S. Leaders continue to navigate these conflicts among their constituents. While DEI programs had faced criticism before this event, the post-attack period saw a significant escalation in opposition, particularly within academic institutions and corporate environments.

Condemning Hamas and supporting retaliation may seem reasonable without considering the complex, longstanding conflict between Middle

Eastern Arab nations and Israel. University campus protests against Israel's response to its conflict with Hamas drew significant media attention. The United States Congress intervened by sending formal requests to three female DEI leaders at elite U.S. universities to defend their responses to "anti-Jewish" sentiment on campuses. It did not go well for the DEI leaders. Dr. Claudine Gay, Harvard's DEI officer and the only Black woman subpoenaed, felt compelled to resign shortly afterward (Krupnik, M. J., 2023). Her resignation was followed by that of Princeton University's DEI officer, Dr. Imani Perry.

Resistance to DEI has often centered on conflicting assumptions about fairness. Proponents advocate for DEI to address systemic inequities that marginalize groups such as BIPOC, women, and immigrants. Their efforts often include affirmative action, quotas, and diversity recruitment to level the playing field. Conversely, critics argue that DEI undermines individual rights and meritocracy, emphasizing personal achievement over collective grievances. High-profile debates, like those between Vivek Ramaswamy and Mark Cuban, highlight these ideological divisions, with Ramaswamy decrying demographic targets as divisive and Cuban defending DEI as a driver of innovation and equity.

Ramaswamy is a biotech entrepreneur and political figure known for criticizing corporate diversity, equity, and inclusion (DEI) initiatives. Cuban is a billionaire entrepreneur and investor who supports DEI efforts, emphasizing their business benefits. In a 2024 episode of The Truth Podcast, Vivek Ramaswamy and Mark Cuban engaged in a spirited discussion about DEI, Environmental, Social, and Governance (ESG) principles, and their broader implications for business and society.

Ramaswamy argues that DEI undermines meritocracy by setting demographic targets that prioritize race, gender, and other group identities over qualifications and abilities. He questioned the effectiveness of these programs, suggesting they might create divisiveness rather than foster unity within organizations. In contrast, Mark Cuban defended the importance of DEI, emphasizing that diversity leads to better decision-making and innovation, which helps organizations better fulfill their mission. He acknowledged the challenges of implementing DEI but stressed that the goal is to create a more equitable environment where individuals from diverse backgrounds can thrive. Cuban further argued that actively seeking talent enhances business performance and improves outcomes.

The two also discussed the government's role in shaping corporate responsibility, with Ramaswamy emphasizing the need to avoid government "overreach," advocating instead for a market-driven approach. While agreeing on the importance of market forces, Cuban highlighted the need for businesses to be socially responsible and adapt to evolving stakeholder expectations. Their exchange reflects the ongoing debate about valuing diversity versus valuing merit in the workplace, illustrating the complexities and differing perspectives on these critical issues.

These challenges underscore the ongoing polarization around DEI as societal debates over fairness, meritocracy, and representation continue to shape its future. The attacks on DEI reflect a deeper cultural struggle with significant implications for the sustainability of inclusion efforts in organizations and institutions. At the core is a zero-sum belief that DEI must address historical injustices or be dismantled entirely. The argument on each side leaves the impression that neither has considered how DEI and organizational success have become intimately intertwined.

The Culture Wars Harm Everyone's Interests

The "us versus them" mentality in reaction to the successful implementation of DEI overlooks the reality that everyone benefits when barriers preventing full participation in society and the economy are identified and removed. When participation barriers exist for any group within an organization, no one experiences full equity. Inequities have significantly contributed to the decline of the American middle class by limiting access to opportunities, perpetuating systemic barriers, and exacerbating economic disparities (Solomon, D., Maxwell, C., & Castro, A., 2019).

Structural barriers, such as unequal access to quality education, healthcare, and affordable housing, disproportionately affect marginalized communities across all cultures. Institutionalized discrimination in hiring, lending practices, and other economic opportunities has historically marginalized certain groups, preventing upward mobility and perpetuating cycles of poverty. Wage stagnation, rising costs of living, and uneven economic growth have disproportionately impacted lower-income and marginalized workers, and shrunk the middle class while wealth gaps increase.

These barriers to equity create disparities in income and wealth accumulation, making it harder for individuals to achieve or maintain a middle-class standard of living. Inequities are embedded in various systems, including education, healthcare, housing, and labor markets, resulting in structural disadvantages that disproportionately affect middle- and lower-income households. Many people attribute the decline of the middle class to factors such as new technologies displacing jobs, poor public education, or unfair competition from affirmative action. While these are undoubtedly important to discuss, this perspective diverts attention from the more insidious institutional barriers.

As wealth becomes increasingly concentrated at the top, economic activity becomes less dynamic, as wealthier households tend to save a larger portion of their income rather than spend it. This trend has also contributed to a polarized job market, where opportunities for well-paying middle-class jobs are declining in favor of low-wage or high-wage positions. This shift stifles upward mobility and creates stagnation for most of the population. Additionally, fewer middle-class households result in reduced tax revenues, limiting funds for public services such as education, healthcare, and infrastructure.

Socially, the erosion of the middle class has undermined mobility, leaving many families with fewer opportunities to improve their economic standing. Children from lower-income families face growing barriers to accessing quality education. Limited resources for homeownership and unstable careers trap them in cycles of limited resources or poverty. The growing gap between the rich and the poor intensifies social tensions and reduces societal cohesion, threatening the fabric of communities and eroding trust in institutions. Political polarization has deepened as economic struggles push people toward more extreme positions in search of solutions, further undermining the democratic process and weakening public confidence in governance (McCoy, J., and Press, B., 2022).

At the community level, the decline of the middle class has destabilized local neighborhoods. Historically, middle-class families have been the backbone of their communities, supporting schools, civic organizations, and small businesses. Their diminishing presence weakens community bonds, reduces access to quality public services, and contributes to urban decline. Housing markets are also affected, as reduced demand for mid-priced homes creates imbalances and leads to higher rates of foreclosures and evictions, further destabilizing communities.

No one wins. Americans share a common interest in ensuring that everyone has access to good-paying jobs, education and training for job readiness, and quality healthcare to help restore the middle class. Businesses also have a stake in this. Middle-class income plays a significant role in consumerism, the economy's heartbeat. The social and economic stability of middle-class jobs is crucial to increased productivity and innovation. In this way, the working class and business owners have an interdependent and harmonious coexistence with diverse perspectives, values, and interests.

More importantly, businesses cannot thrive when the workplace hierarchy reflects society's socioeconomic stratification. The public transit workplace is an example. In modern, culturally diverse cities, the workers in the most vulnerable and thankless jobs tend to be recent immigrants, BIPOCs, and women. Yet, these workers often hold the most critical jobs. A city's public transportation system would come to a near halt without bus operators who serve the public daily. Those at the bottom of the organizational chart are more likely to feel the brunt of attacks on DEI and the resulting economic consequences. This is why racial equity must take center stage in our approach to the work. When there is no equity, no one in the organization thoroughly enjoys it.

Creative Coexistence

Basecamp is a small software company known for its project management tools and applications. In April 2021, the leadership announced a controversial internal policy change: the CEO banned "societal and political discussions" on its workplace communication channels. The company argued that political and social debates were distracting and insisted that Basecamp employees should focus solely on work.

The decision came amidst ongoing discussions around DEI BPs and employee demands for corporate social responsibility, both of which had intensified across the U.S. following the social justice movements of 2020. Like many companies, Basecamp employees engaged in racial equity, diversity initiatives, and political conversations, reflecting a broader cultural shift toward openly discussing social issues at work. Basecamp leadership reportedly felt that these conversations created divisiveness, prompting them to implement the policy change. The leadership also eliminated its commitment to DEI, disbanding the DEI committee and shifting the focus to individual responsibility rather than implementing DEI BPs. Some maternal leave benefits and a practice allowing employees to give each other feedback were also curtailed (Griffith, E., 2021).

The announcement led to an immediate employee backlash, particularly from those who supported the DEI BP initiative. Many viewed the new policy as a step backward, expressing frustration and feeling that it was an effort to silence historically marginalized and excluded group employees and social justice advocates' voices within the company. The ban on social justice discussions was perceived as an attempt to stifle dialogue on racial justice, equity, and other vital topics that impacted them. Within days of the announcement, about one-third of Basecamp's fifty-seven employees chose to resign, including several senior employees who had been with the company for years.

Basecamp's decision to restrict DEI discussions and remove DEI BPs had lasting effects on its reputation. Once known as a progressive, employee-focused company, Basecamp's brand was now associated with regression in its commitment to inclusion, potentially limiting its appeal to diverse talent. The incident led to introspection among other companies navigating similar tensions, with some doubling down on their DEI commitments and others reconsidering how social issues fit within their corporate culture. While Basecamp survived the controversy, the reputational hit remains, particularly among professionals who value DEI. As a private company, there is no available data to determine the full impact of the changes. However, the company has seen reduced industry influence compared to its earlier days. Losing top engineers and product leaders has slowed innovation and affected long-term growth.

The Basecamp incident highlights the challenges of managing workplace culture in a society grappling with institutionalized inequity and an increasingly socially conscious workforce. It serves as a cautionary case study for organizations balancing productivity with creating inclusive, socially engaged workspaces. While Basecamp continues to operate, the long-term implications of its 2021 policy changes remain a subject of discussion. The incident serves as a case study of the importance of balancing alignment with company policies, employee values, societal expectations, and government regulations. It also highlights how internal decisions can have far-reaching consequences for employee morale, innovation, client relationships, and overall brand reputation.

Historically, employee engagement focused on productivity and job satisfaction. Today, employees seek purpose-driven roles that align with their values and contribute to broader social missions. Organizations that emphasize corporate social responsibility, sustainability, and ethical practices aim to attract and retain talent. Alongside meaningful work, professional development, strong leadership, workplace relationships, and fair compensation are key drivers of engagement. Companies that adapt to these priorities can foster motivated, productive teams and achieve long-term success.

Finding ways to enhance employee engagement requires understanding the workforce's values and how the organization's values and objectives align with them. Certified B Corporations, companies with strong social responsibility programs, environmentally focused NGOs, and social enterprises are among the leading organizations that attract employees who prioritize social responsibility. Today, every organization is expected to have a DEI solution to remain competitive. A balance between workforce needs and institutional goals must be achieved to stay relevant in the market. While competitive pay is undoubtedly important, employees are often willing to accept a tradeoff in their salary for better work-life balance and alignment with corporate values. This is where creative coexistence comes into play.

According to the late Buddhist leader Daisaku Ikeda, who coined the term "creative coexistence," businesses and their employees are not merely in a transactional relationship where labor is exchanged for wages. Instead, they share a deep, interdependent relationship that requires teamwork for the organization's and society's greater good. This book uniquely assumes a creative coexistence relationship between an organization's business goals and the culturally diverse talent needed to achieve them. While the workforce and business interests may have become increasingly oppositional, their symbiotic relationship cannot be denied. Creative coexistence emphasizes mutual respect, collaboration, and a shared commitment to achieving both workforce and organizational goals.

When business and the workforce operate based on coexistence values, mutual respect and recognition of each other's inherent dignity take center stage. Employers view their employees as valuable partners, not just as a means to an end. Similarly, employees see their work as meaningful and contributing to the overall mission and success of the organization. Employees prefer working for organizations that have an impact on their communities and society as a whole (Weir, K., 2024). As a consultant, it is disappointing when employees cannot quickly and accurately identify their collective mission. Across hundreds of training sessions, we have conducted, transit bus operators in a large metropolitan transit agency consistently state that their collective mission is to get their paycheck or get home safely. Yet, they wholeheartedly agree when I remind them that their collective mission is to get people safely, effectively, and efficiently from where they board to their destination.

Bus operators are the backbone of carrying out a transit agency's mission. A transit agency's talent management strategy must involve learning about and addressing obstacles that make it difficult for bus operators to accomplish their mission. Understanding how each level of the organization, from frontline workers to executives, coexists with and depends on the others can inspire the collaboration needed to solve problems together. This is especially true when a transit agency faces difficulties with service breakdowns and poor customer service.

Creative coexistence in the workplace involves aligning business goals with the needs and aspirations of employees. Daisaku Ikeda emphasizes developing a shared vision in which both the organization and workforce strive toward common objectives that contribute to economic success and social responsibility, helping the larger society in which they coexist. This alignment fosters a mutual sense of purpose and belonging, motivating employees to contribute more meaningfully to the organization. In turn, the organization invests in and supports its workforce, creating a cycle of growth and commitment. A high-impact cultural diversity, equity, and inclusion initiative aims to develop a creative coexistence approach to aligning workforce and business goals.

Navigating the Legal Minefield:
Sustaining DEI Without Sacrificing Fairness

However, working toward mutual benefit in a polarized DEI environment is challenged by opposing deeply entrenched views and poor execution. Here are some key challenges to getting opposing parties to adopt a creative coexistence perspective:

1. Confirmation Bias: People often overemphasize information that supports their beliefs while discrediting evidence that contradicts them. Those who view DEI as divisive or discriminatory tend to seek out data or arguments that reinforce this perspective and dismiss contrary facts as biased or invalid. This makes it difficult for them to entertain the possibility that the opposing view may have merit or accept a balanced view that considers both sides. When presented with alternative viewpoints, individuals tend to reject factual information that conflicts with their entrenched views, resulting in each party believing that the other is unwilling to learn "the truth." This is also a problem for those blindly in favor of DEI. They are less likely to compassionately view the impact on the historically majority groups. Both discount the pain that the other group experiences.

2. Misinformation and Misinterpretation of Data: Both sides selectively use statistics or facts, leading to misleading arguments. For example, proponents of DEI may highlight studies showing that diverse teams are more innovative and productive, while opponents focus on data suggesting that certain DEI practices (like quotas) lead to reverse discrimination. The challenge is to ensure that (1) data is interpreted in its proper context and not manipulated to fit a particular agenda and (2) both supporting and opposing data are taken into consideration.

3. Emotional and Ideological Attachments: Many people hold deeply emotional or ideological attachments to their views on DEI. Those who see it as an asset to organizations often argue from justice and inclusion perspectives, while those who view it as divisive may see it as a threat to fairness or merit. Emotional reactions can cloud logical

reasoning and create barriers to healthy debate and understanding (Vaughn, B. E. (2002). When emotions are involved, facts alone may be insufficient to change someone's perspective without addressing opposing values and beliefs.

4. Legal and Constitutional Arguments: Opposition to DEI often involves legal claims, such as references to reverse discrimination or the constitutionality of affirmative action. Legal precedents, such as those set in Supreme Court cases (e.g., Grutter v. Bollinger or Students for Fair Admissions v. Harvard), become deeply entrenched in discussions about what is just from a legal perspective, adding another layer of complexity to the debate. Conversations are undermined when DEI advocates interpret court decisions differently from the opposition, especially when the decisions are viewed as politically motivated.

5. Perception of DEI as a Zero-Sum Game: Some opponents perceive DEI policies as a zero-sum game, believing that DEI initiatives benefit certain groups at the expense of others, particularly in hiring or admissions practices. This belief makes it difficult to present DEI as a tool for mutual benefit, as opponents may view it as a threat to their opportunities. This mindset requires a shift in how DEI is framed, emphasizing its potential to benefit all members of society and organizations. The challenge arises when the opposition is deeply rooted in a different worldview.

6. Evolving Social Norms: While most workers agree that promoting DEI in organizations to treat people fairly is a good thing, they differ on what fairness means and how to institutionalize it. Even DEI advocates disagree on how to create fairness. The equity versus equality debate often relies on assumptions about the benefits of diversity, equity, and inclusion for organizations (e.g., improved performance, better decision-making, more innovation), as well as broader societal benefits (e.g., addressing systemic inequalities). However, these social norms and values are still evolving. Younger generations tend to view DEI as common sense or simply just (e.g., striving for inclusivity), while older generations may

see it as having run its course. This generational divide can make facts seem less persuasive to those holding more traditional views, who may view current DEI trends as transient or misguided.

7. <u>Language and Framing:</u> The way facts and data are framed matters. Opponents of DEI often argue that practices like quotas or preferential treatment based on race violate the principle of merit-based decisions. It is unhelpful for proponents to defend preferential treatment as a solution to address past harm, even if it may be just. This argument often clashes with entrenched American values of equality. Instead, raising questions about the existence of merit, such as discussing university admissions that favor legacy connections regardless of merit, may encourage critical thinking. The challenge lies in using inclusive language that resonates with different audiences while avoiding polarizing or inflammatory terms that could further entrench opposing views. Asking critical thinking questions is one effective approach.

So, how do we foster a dialog based on a creative coexistence approach?

To engage effectively, focus on shared values. Empathetically acknowledge the other side's concerns to foster respectful dialogue and avoid alienation. Present facts as part of a broader narrative about societal improvement and long-term benefits for all. Use terms that reflect values everyone shares, such as fairness, equal opportunity, and addressing systemic barriers. Share compelling case studies or success stories from organizations that have seen improvements in employee satisfaction, innovation, and performance through DEI programs.

Suppose your goal is to help an opponent understand that DEI may have been executed in ways that ran legally afoul, but it has sound legal standing overall. The main challenge is entrenched opposition. To help them appreciate that you share views, approach the conversation with empathy, clear context, and a focus on shared values. A memorandum by a group of legal scholars is an example of data that reduces resistance.

Here is a summary of the memorandum, DEI Programs Are Lawful Under Federal Civil Rights Laws and Supreme Court Precedent, written by a group of legal scholars. The memorandum argues that institutions have the legal right to engage in their First Amendment-protected speech and points out how this is explicitly recognized in the January 21, 2025, presidential executive order (Rice, D., et al., 2025). The order also states that it "does not prevent State or local governments, Federal contractors, or federally funded state and local educational agencies or institutions of higher education from engaging in First Amendment protected speech." This means that universities and organizations can continue to express their commitment to DEI through various means, such as using these terms on their websites and publications or displaying supportive messages on campus. To engage effectively, focus on their common mission, purpose, and commitment. Empathetically acknowledge the other side's concerns to foster respectful dialogue and avoid alienation. Present facts as part of a broader narrative about societal improvement and long-term benefits for all. Use terms that reflect values everyone shares, such as fairness, equal opportunity, and addressing systemic barriers. Share compelling case studies or success stories from organizations that have seen improvements in employee satisfaction, innovation, and performance through DEI programs. Transit personnel have unique views of their concerns and needs depending on their level in the organization, but they are all committed to, and take pride in, doing the best job possible to transport passengers safely, effectively, and efficiently.

Suppose your goal is to help an opponent understand that although DEI may have been executed in ways that ran legally afoul, it has sound legal standing overall. The main challenge is entrenched opposition. To help them appreciate your shared views, approach the conversation with empathy, clear context, and a focus on shared values. A memorandum by a group of legal scholars is an example of data that reduces resistance.

Here is a summary of the memorandum, DEI Programs Are Lawful Under Federal Civil Rights Laws and Supreme Court Precedent, written by the group of legal scholars (Rice, D., et al., 2025). The memorandum makes the case that institutions have the legal right to engage in their First Amendment-protected speech and point out how that is explicitly recognized in the January 21, 2025, presidential executive order (Rice, D., et al., 2025, February 20). The order also states that it "does not prevent State or local governments, Federal contractors, or Federally funded State and local educational agencies or institutions of higher education from engaging in First Amendment protected speech. This means that universities and organizations can continue to express their commitment to DEI through various means, such as using these terms on their websites and publications or displaying supportive messages on campus.

The authors list examples of DEI practices that do not involve racial classification, which they acknowledge the courts have justifiably deemed illegal under the Fourteenth Amendment. According to their collective professional opinion, these include:

- Positively crediting an individual's personal experiences with or demonstrated ability to remedy various forms of systemic discrimination, such as anti-Black racism or anti-LGBTQ bigotry, in admissions and hiring decisions.
- University programming or events that focus on identity groups or societal bias, but remain open to all students.
- Affinity groups or themed residence halls that foreground a particular group or identity while remaining accessible to all students.
- Designing anti-harassment training that equips campus stakeholders to confront implicit biases and societal stereotypes.
- Tracking applicants' racial and gender identities to assess the aggregate impact of hiring or admissions processes.
- Taking affirmative steps to mitigate unjustifiable disparities and inequities in hiring or admissions contexts.

- Adopting admissions or hiring criteria to racially integrate historically HMIG universities, such as eliminating legacy preferences.
- Investing in professional and impartial internal investigation units to respond to complaints of bias or discrimination.
- Proclaiming a commitment to cultivating an inclusive campus environment where all students feel valued.
- Investing in academic departments and curricula that foreground the experiences of specific racial or ethnic groups.
- Adopting policies that promote full inclusion and accessibility for all community members, regardless of ability status.
- Providing "all gender" restrooms available to all campus community members.
- Implementing recruitment and retention programs that focus on the experiences of specific groups but are available to all.

These initiatives promote diversity, equity, and inclusion without employing racial classifications, thereby remaining legally secure under federal civil rights laws.

Notice that the memorandum acknowledges that some attacks on DEI were justified, yet corrected by recent court decisions. It also asserts that the core principles of fairness and justice remain intact, enabling progress toward overcoming institutional inequities that most people continue to value. In a conversation with someone opposed to DEI, acknowledging that racial quotas are unlawful and emphasizing the shared value of treating people justly can help affirm their opposition to DEI while justifying continued DEI support. This makes them less argumentative. Additionally, clarifying misconceptions, such as the idea that recent court decisions make DEI illegal, can open a dialogue that encourages support for diverse viewpoints and reduces resistance to DEI. Providing them with additional data and articles about DEI will be helpful once they are open to learning and sharing without feeling that the conversation is oppositional.

This book's approach is based on the idea that no one can be left behind in DEI work. Opposition to DEI is not a threat but a starting point for dialogue and increased understanding if the practitioner is willing to listen deeply to what is behind the opposition and point out mutual benefits. They must also be prepared to embrace differences and adequately prepare for dialogue to increase understanding.

Chapter 3: The Diversity Best Practice Dilemma

Many cultural diversity professionals enter their roles with minimal, if any, experience, related education or professional training. Their approach is to implement popular DEI BPs because these practices are well-accepted and tangible. Consider Maria, an African American salesperson at a medical technology company. As the only African American in a predominantly HMIG workplace, Maria earned recognition as a talented sales trainer with a strong track record of championing DEI initiatives. Due to her success in sales and her strong organizational fit, Maria's CEO recruited her to lead a newly created DEI position. This is a common pathway to DEI roles, reflecting the lack of expertise needed to secure such positions.

Upon assuming her new role, Maria engaged with various management and departmental teams within the organization to assess prior diversity and inclusion efforts and to determine present needs. She also connected with online and local professional networks focused on cultural diversity, gleaning valuable insights. Through her research, Maria learned what competitors in her industry were doing with their DEI programs. She learned the importance of developing a business case for DEI, which she developed and submitted to her CEO for consideration. However, she did not have a staff or a budget and was uncertain whether these resources were necessary.

The company funded the implementation of various "diversity best practices" to foster an inclusive and equitable work environment. The best practices included:

- Cultural awareness training
- Diversity recruitment strategies
- Forming employee resource groups to offer different identity groups a safe place to congregate

- Community outreach and charitable contribution activities
- Implementing equal pay policies
- Implementing leadership development programs for women

A couple of years later, Diversity Officer Magazine praised the company and Maria for their efforts to promote a diverse workforce and cultivate an inclusive work environment. The magazine featured an article about her work, and her photo appeared on the cover. The company's initiative received recognition through awards, and it was hailed as a model for others in its sector, making notable progress toward its DEI goals. However, despite these sincere efforts, a discrimination allegation surfaced from a relatively new Black employee, who complained of unequal treatment in job responsibilities and compensation compared to HMIG colleagues.

The company recognized the seriousness of the claims and launched a comprehensive internal review to identify and understand the barriers to fairness faced by Black employees. This crucial step aimed to make necessary changes to address the identified inequities more effectively.

Maria wisely hired a reputable external consultant to conduct the investigation. By involving an external expert, the investigation could be conducted objectively, allowing for a full and fair evaluation of the situation. The company and Maria demonstrated their commitment to addressing the allegations and finding a resolution. The investigation report revealed that, despite the organization's pronounced commitment to inclusion, evidence of unfair treatment and racial marginalization remained. The African American employee was upset that the company had received diversity awards while their complaints about unfairness had been reported. They also felt that the concerns of HMIG female employees were taken more seriously. Despite the significant effort and resources invested in diversity best practices, the perception of racial inequity persisted, something that neither the CEO nor Maria could fully comprehend. They were taken aback by the extent of the racism described by the employee based on their experiences.

Implementing the strategic plan required major changes to long-standing talent management policies and practices. Initially, the organization took swift action to address the employee's complaint, pausing legal proceedings and demonstrating a commitment to change. However, resistance from upper management stalled progress, leading the employee's attorneys to resume formal action.

The situation intensified when the lawsuit was reinstated and hit the media shortly thereafter. This prompted the company's Board of Directors to scrutinize the efficacy of implementing DEI and its resulting legal vulnerabilities. In response, the CEO felt compelled to take action, which led to Maria's unfortunate resignation. This left Maria feeling betrayed and questioning her future as a DEI practitioner, especially given the potential damage to her reputation.

What could Maria have done differently to protect herself and the organization? She had been careful to deploy the DEI BPs that her colleagues at other organizations used. Although these practices were aimed at promoting inclusion, implementing DEI BPs led many HMIG employees to perceive the initiatives as quotas or a dilution of talent. Some saw the DEI program as fundamentally unfair and divisive. The African American employee who filed the lawsuit felt that the DEI program should have protected them. While DEI BPs may appear to be an ideal solution on the surface, they can fall short when they are not data-driven and part of a larger strategy designed for profound impact. But how can a company with these awards get into legal jeopardy?

The Diversity Best Practice Award Deception

Receiving recognition for implementing DEI BPs is undoubtedly worthwhile. It highlights an organization's dedication to creating a diverse, equitable, and inclusive workplace. Awards can provide public recognition, boost employee morale, and attract talented individuals who value these principles. However, the downside is that DEI awards primarily focus on acknowledging a company's commitment and the best practices it has in place rather than evaluating their effectiveness. Evaluators must rely on the applicant's self-report rather than independently scrutinizing the organization's records, policies, and procedures. Best practices showcase an organization's tangible efforts to promote DEI, measuring how many practices have been implemented based on the belief that an organization's culture becomes more inclusive and equitable once these practices are integrated into daily operations.

DEI BPs, such as diversity recruitment and employee resource groups, tend to be based on an equality approach. These initiatives provide the same opportunities and resources to everyone, regardless of their readiness to fully take advantage of them. It is also noteworthy that these awards reinforce the adoption of equality-based practices that promote quotas, which can expose organizations to legal risks, rather than solutions that implement DEI initiatives in ways that provide legal protection. The result is that equality approaches to DEI often fall short of addressing systemic barriers or tailoring support to meet the specific needs of historically marginalized and excluded groups—a nuance that traditional approaches tend not to address.

L'Oréal is an example. It consistently received diversity awards for exceptional DEI practices and progress (L'Oréal USA, (n.d.). The personal care company, with tens of thousands of employees worldwide, consistently received diversity awards for exceptional DEI practices and progress. In March 2023, L'Oréal successfully defended itself against a lawsuit filed by a former vice president, who alleged that her termination was due to racial and mental health discrimination. In 2021, a different lawsuit was filed against L'Oréal, in which the claimant accused the company of race, sex, and disability discrimination. There were also previous allegations dating back to 2003 and 2007 for age discrimination and racial discrimination, respectively. L'Oréal is not alone.

Wells Fargo, a prominent financial institution, has also received multiple DEI BP awards. However, it has faced scrutiny and lawsuits over allegations of discrimination against BIPOC communities. In one instance from 2017, Wells Fargo was under legal scrutiny for allegedly preying on HMEG communities for economic gain while receiving an award for its diversity initiatives in the same week (Rosenbaum, E., 2017).

The news stories about award-winning companies being sued for discrimination highlight the hard facts about many DEI initiatives. While some progress has been made, the organizations most well-known for conferring diversity best practice awards continue to rely primarily on self-assessment report data for their competition. Organizations that confer DEI awards do not have a verification process that ensures the applicants are honest. Additionally, the application fee to enter the competition can be as high as $15,000, depending on the organization's size. Such a financial relationship raises questions about the objectivity of these ranking decisions, especially when they are based solely on self-reported data.

The fact that a potential awardee could be undergoing a discrimination lawsuit during the award application process—while not being required to disclose it—raises concerns about the decision-making process. While it is important to avoid punishing organizations merely for allegations, shouldn't existing DEI-related legal challenges be transparent and considered before ranking the competition? If legal problems are discovered during verification, what decision-making criteria allow those organizations to rank high even after it is revealed they are under a discrimination lawsuit?

Demonstrating success in meeting diversity hiring quotas, offering diversity training, and ensuring access to mentoring opportunities are practices implemented from the perspective that the organization has not provided equal access. What has mattered most is that the best practices showcase the organization's commitment to branding and competing for awards.

Addressing the Limitations of Diversity Best Practices

Organizational leaders understand that there is a talent shortage, and today, the existing talent pool is increasingly culturally diverse. They are also recognizing that developing a long-term cultural diversity and inclusion strategy is critical to remaining competitive and increasing market share. Leaders are aware of diversity best practice awards and the advantage they offer over competitor firms, particularly in profitability measures. While the benefits for a handful of Fortune 50 companies are laudable, there remains room for a broader, more significant impact overall.

It may feel safer to utilize existing best practices that competitors have implemented, but that does not necessarily make it a wise decision. The organization can better manage change and risk by shifting from equality to equity. Creating an equitable organization, compared to one based on equality, is challenging because it requires profound cultural change. Organizations tend to resist cultural change even when it is in their best interest to do so. Culture change is difficult and disruptive. Organizations resist cultural change due to fear of the unknown and a lack of understanding of what change would look like, as change disrupts established customs and workflows, forcing the workforce out of its comfort zone. Loss of control and concerns about job security also contribute to resistance, as employees may worry about how changes will affect their roles and livelihoods. Additionally, changes in job descriptions, routines, and team dynamics can cause discomfort and insecurity. Psychological attachment to the current way of doing things and a lack of trust in the change process can further entrench resistance.

Perhaps the most crucial factor that underscores the need for deeper intervention is that those at the bottom of the organizational hierarchy tend to view DEI BPs as less impactful than those at higher levels. Studies have shown that the efficacy of diversity and inclusion practices is often linked to employees' perspectives on implementation.

In scrutinizing demographic variances in workers' opinions at notable best practice award-winning companies, the National Urban League's studies uncovered significant contrasts. The surveys gauged employee perceptions of the impact of the companies' diversity initiatives by having respondents rate their organization's practices from "effective" to "less effective." While overall feedback about the organization's DEI efforts was positive, it emerged that Black employees and younger workers aged 18-34 expressed notably less satisfaction, even at top-rated award-winning companies (National Urban League, 2005; National Urban League. (2009).

The Urban League's Diversity at Work report and its subsequent companion publication reveal a critical insight: African American employees are less likely than other groups to perceive their company's diversity best practice award positively compared to other workforce segments. This difference suggests that using cumulative data to assess DEI success does not provide the full picture. What appears to be success is not resonating with those who face systemic inequities the most. The perspectives of African Americans, employees with disabilities, LGBTQIA+, and other HMEG employees serve as a crucial litmus test for accurately measuring equity within an organization. If DEI initiatives do not align with the standards or lived realities of the groups historically suffering from workplace inequities and exclusion, the initiative falls short of its intended goals. Therefore, a workplace's ability to achieve meaningful equity must be assessed based on the experiences of its most marginalized employees. Evaluations from groups, such as African Americans, are key to testing DEI success. If they do not experience equity, then everyone in the organization is falling short, even if they are unaware.

Research conducted by McKinsey & Company and the Society for Human Resource Management (SHRM) shed further light on African American employees' perceptions of the workplace. McKinsey conducted extensive research to understand the experience of African American employees in the U.S. workplace. They analyzed data from various sources, including the U.S. Bureau of Labor Statistics, the U.S. Census Bureau, and twenty-four companies representing 3.7 million U.S. employees. The findings highlighted the significant challenges that Black workers face in feeling included in the workplace (McKinsey & Company. (2021).

Some of the key findings from the McKinsey research included:

- Disparities in Overall Industry Concentration: Nearly half of Black U.S. workers are concentrated in industries with a significant frontline service presence, such as healthcare, retail, accommodations, public transit, and food service. This industry concentration impacts factors like wages, career advancement, and the risk of displacement due to economic disruption. Conversely, Black workers are underrepresented in higher-wage industries like architecture, finance, and law. These disparities contribute to a broader sense of inequality.

- Promotion and Leadership Disparities: Black U.S. employees often face an upside-down organizational pyramid. They are highly represented at the bottom, but a disproportionately small number ascend to higher levels within the organization. This results from lower promotion rates from entry-level to managerial positions compared to their counterparts. The disparity contributes to the lack of Black leadership within companies, highlighting the need to address representation at the senior levels. While some progress has been made in increasing Black representation on corporate boards, representation in the most senior ranks of many companies remains limited. Black workers often perceive the overrepresentation at the bottom and the scarcity of leaders who look like them at the top, along with fewer promotions, as "more of the same inequities" they have long been accustomed to.

- Trust Deficit: Black workers often perceive a significant trust deficit in the workplace, particularly concerning their acceptance, authenticity, and values. They frequently feel that their employers view them as a diversity statistic rather than valuing their talent. One individual shared in a training I conducted that their public sector organization claims higher education is the key to upward mobility. Yet, despite receiving a master's degree, the worker remained at the supervisor level after numerous unsuccessful promotion applications.

The group continues to lack trust in the organization's ability to change these circumstances for them individually and as a group.

SHRM conducted a study that examined perceptions of racial inequity among African Americans and historically majority groups and included group workers in the workplace. The study, conducted in June 2020, revealed significant differences in perceptions between these two groups:

- Perceptions of Discrimination: While 35% of African American workers agreed that discrimination based on race or ethnicity exists in their workplace, only 7% of historically majority and included group workers agreed. This disparity reflects a significant difference in how different racial groups experience the workplace (SHRM, 2020).

- Perceptions of Workplace Efforts: Regarding workplace efforts to promote racial justice, 29% of HMIG workers felt that their workplace was not doing enough. In comparison, more than 50% of African American workers shared this sentiment. Interestingly, both racial groups were equally uncomfortable when engaging in candid conversations about race at work.

African Americans are not alone. Research on women's perceptions of inequities they experience suggests that much more is needed to place them in positions of authority, and they are more likely to experience pay disparities compared to men in the same job roles (Sieghart, M. A., 2024, November 15; Eagly, A. H., & Karau, S. J., 2002). These findings support the Urban League's research conclusions regarding the variations in how workplace DEI BPs are perceived.

The studies highlight the significance of advancement opportunities and the overall experience of HMEG African American workers in shaping their trust in organizations. Methods for promoting equity and inclusion will become more effective when the experiences and needs of HMEG employees are referenced as a key measure of those practices' success. The implications for talent management and productivity improvement cannot be overstated.

DEI practitioners vary in their approach, views about the work, and assumptions. Some aim to level the playing field, while others strive to rectify injustices and empower the disadvantaged. Promoting an organization's commitment to DEI through best practices is beneficial when legal risks are mitigated; however, chasing awards can make it challenging to identify equity barriers and address deep-rooted cultural practices. Actual change requires a foundational shift in organizational culture, which is not reflected in winning diversity awards.

This book introduces the ECDI framework for organizational change. This framework fosters a sustainable environment where inclusion, productivity, and engagement thrive among employees, underpinned by a culture of equity that enhances their productivity and involvement.

Challenges in DEI Initiative Execution

Implementing DEI is a common first step when an organization begins this journey. To achieve meaningful outcomes, leaders must navigate the complex landscape of support and resistance shaped by perceptions, assumptions, and execution pitfalls. Below are the key challenges organizations face in executing DEI efforts and their implications. They include: (1) historically majority and included group perceptions of DEI as fairness, (2) blaming, shaming and complaining about historically majority and included groups, (3) including only historically marginalized and excluded groups on the DEI equity and inclusion competency committees and working groups, and (4) poor DEI leadership inclusion competencies.

A frequent challenge in DEI execution is the perception of unfairness among historically majority and included groups when resources like mentorship programs or leadership development are allocated exclusively to historically marginalized and excluded groups. While these programs are often designed to address systemic barriers, it is understandable that historically majority and included group employees feel excluded or undervalued when the DEI emphasizes lifting up historically marginalized and excluded groups. This perception undermines the initiative's stated goals of fostering inclusion when there is resentment or skepticism toward the efforts. A truly inclusive approach requires balancing targeted interventions with broader strategies that ensure all employees feel valued and supported.

Another obstacle is the tendency for individuals to make broad assumptions about a group's privilege based on their racial or ethnic identity. While privilege is a crucial concept in understanding systemic inequities, it can overlook the nuanced and unique experiences of individuals when overgeneralized. For instance, a historically majority and included group employee may still face significant personal challenges, such as economic hardship or disability, that affect their workplace experience. In any case, no one appreciates being labeled, blamed, or shamed, even when it aims to highlight essential sources of differences. People need to feel appreciated, even if they agree with the intention behind the initiative. Overlooking or discounting their perspective can alienate employees and detract from the core DEI mission of ensuring fairness and understanding for all.

DEI is often seen as an effort focused solely on specific historically marginalized and excluded groups, which can unintentionally exclude others from DEI committees or initiatives. For instance, forming a DEI committee often signals to employees that only members of historically marginalized and excluded groups are invited to participate. When the committee is comprised mostly of members of historically marginalized groups, such as BIPOCS, it conveys to other employees that DEI is going to benefit only historically marginalized and excluded group employees, especially when they feel that their input is left out of the planning process. This perception of exclusion limits historically majority and included group support and acceptance, ultimately reducing the effectiveness of DEI implementation. That is why including a cross-section of the entire organization represents a successful DEI initiative. The cultural diversity makes it more challenging to align everyone, but that is inherent in the work.

The effectiveness of any DEI initiative is closely linked to leadership competencies. Unfortunately, many DEI leaders are underprepared or lack the necessary skills to implement complex, organization-wide changes. This often stems from being hired internally from another role or a limited understanding of the extensive training required for preparation. Skills such as inclusion competency, conflict resolution, mediation, and the ability to identify and address barriers to fairness are crucial, yet they may not always be present among DEI leaders. Poor practitioner competency can result in poorly designed initiatives, employee resistance, and a loss of trust in the organization's commitment to DEI. Investing in the development of DEI leadership competencies is vital to overcoming this challenge.

The path to effective DEI execution is fraught with challenges, but recognizing and addressing these pitfalls is critical to success. Organizations must strike a balance between targeted support for marginalized groups and creating an environment where all employees feel included. By moving beyond broad assumptions, fostering inclusion in DEI initiative implementation, and ensuring strong leadership competencies, organizations can build a more equitable and inclusive workplace. When executed strategically, implementing DEI can be positioned to transform organizational culture.

Implementing DEI BPs is Insufficient to Affect Organizational Culture Change

DEI BPs are essential for promoting equity and inclusion, but they often fail to address the deeply embedded values, beliefs, taboos, and practices that prevent cultural change. They frequently implement solutions haphazardly and struggle to integrate them into everyday practices. Instead of fostering lasting change, they often reinforce inequities by prioritizing inclusion practices that help historically marginalized and excluded group members feel included while overlooking the systemic issues at the core of the problem. Multicultural holiday celebrations, employee resource groups, and diversity training are common examples of surface-level activities (Vaughn, 2008). DEI BPs work best when they target specific equity challenges, especially those affecting historically marginalized and excluded groups. For instance, why provide training in managing diversity if data shows that employees struggle with unclear paths to upward mobility and scarce mentoring opportunities? Developing procedures to create a clear path to promotions will fall short of addressing equity if they result in what is perceived as an exclusive club for historically marginalized and excluded groups.

Specifically, relying solely on diversity best practices often maintains the status quo in organizations rather than driving meaningful cultural change. Here are several reasons why:

1. Short-Term Focus: Many diversity training programs focus on short-term awareness training and compliance rather than long-term behavioral change and shifts in organizational practices, policies, and procedures. This often results in adjustments based on external influences (e.g., the George Floyd protests or a court equal opportunity decision) that do not lead to sustained improvements in the workforce's sense of equity.

2. Lack of Systemic Change: Best practices often fail to address deeper, systemic issues within an organization's culture. For example,

mandatory racial equity training may be delivered to the lower levels of the organization without holding middle management accountable for attendance. While raising awareness of inequities, this approach can increase complaints and legal threats without addressing the structural changes needed to achieve a broader sense of fairness.

3. <u>Insufficient Leadership Engagement</u>: Effective diversity initiatives require active involvement and commitment from leadership. Without this, DEI efforts remain superficial and fail to permeate the organizational culture. Too often, leaders offer lip service to the organization's DEI efforts while distancing themselves from the implementation process and inner workings of the initiatives.

4. <u>Overemphasis on Increasing Historically Marginalized and Excluded Group Numbers to Achieve Cultural Diversity</u>: While diversity metrics are essential, focusing solely on numbers can lead to tokenism rather than true equity. Organizations might hire diverse employees to meet targets without creating an environment where these employees feel valued and can thrive. This is particularly problematic when the ultimate goal is to win a diversity best practice award competition, which often enhances brand identity but also creates legal liabilities.

5. <u>Exclusion of Broader Cultural Norms</u>: DEI BPs often overlook the importance of broader cultural norms and policies that may inadvertently exclude historically marginalized and excluded groups. Effective DEI efforts require identifying sources of inequities and revising organizational policies, procedures, and practices to foster genuine inclusion. For example, a transit agency struggled with disparities in how African American women were disciplined despite years of complaints. The issue was rooted in upper management's reluctance to change policies, relying instead on a generic equal opportunity policy.

6. <u>Misunderstanding the Differences Between Equality and Equity in Achieving Fairness</u>: An organization that promotes equality without dismantling barriers to equity cannot fully develop a culture of fairness. Efforts to recruit one woman or BIPOC individual, for instance, into

a senior position without a genuine commitment to identifying and removing the obstacles that necessitated the initiative will not bring about meaningful change.

7. Understanding the Distinction Between Equality-Based Best Practices and Equity-Based Solutions: Staying ahead of the rapidly changing demographic landscape requires companies to understand equity and how to create it in talent management. Addressing systemic inequities and fostering a culture of inclusion requires an approach that goes beyond equality-based practices to include equity-driven solutions.

Challenges for Addressing the Demographic Shift

Cultural diversity disrupts traditional organizational hierarchies, necessitating effective talent management. As demographic shifts reshape the global workforce and consumer landscape, companies are grappling with adapting to a more diverse and inclusive talent pool. While this shift presents opportunities for innovation and growth, it also introduces significant challenges that can hinder progress if left unaddressed. Organizations must contend with resistance to change, entrenched biases that obstruct the acceptance of differences, and the daunting task of aligning products and services to fully capitalize on evolving demographics. Additionally, gaps in DEI strategies that fall short of full inclusion, coupled with technology and accessibility barriers, further complicate efforts to remain relevant and competitive. This requires innovative DEI approaches.

The key challenges innovative DEI practitioners face, particularly when their work conflicts with traditional values, include: (1) deploying an organizational change strategy, (2) managing resistance to change, (3) addressing lingering biases against and attacks on DEI, and (4) integrating DEI strategy into the organization's mission and operations. Traditional approaches to DEI goals lag behind legal and political changes, rendering them obsolete in an era of global and national transformation. This highlights the need to rethink traditional practices and mindsets to address the urgent need for creating equitable organizations.

By examining the roots of these challenges, we can gain actionable insights for building a more equitable and forward-thinking approach. However, providing a new framework will not be readily embraced. Modern DEI approaches must balance the necessary changes to disrupt outdated practices and become more equity-centered, supporting business goals. While DEI BPs are well-accepted go-to solutions, their benefits are insufficient to meet the needs of the current climate, as noted. Fortunately, the need for managing talent in culturally diverse organizations and the current knowledge-sharing economy offer opportunities for rethinking the case for DEI.

The Need for Reimagining DEI as a Strategic Imperative

A newly appointed chief diversity officer (CDO) at a billion-dollar, family-owned medical device company engaged my company, Diversity Training University International (DTUI.com), to create the company's first DEI initiative. I summarized the return on investment (ROI) for implementing the initiative during an initial meeting with the company president. The president responded by stating that ROI was not important. Their commitment to DEI was driven by the belief that it was "the right thing to do." While admirable, this perspective highlighted their lack of strategic alignment and understanding of DEI's broader business benefits. Another concern was that DEI was being treated as charitable giving.

The CDO applied the insights she gained from our Diversity Executive Leadership Academy's certification training program to create a tailored business case for DEI that aligned with the company's needs.

However, the president refused to allow the collection of survey data necessary to assess the organization's needs. After presenting the business case to the leadership team, the CDO requested an annual budget to support the initiative and other essential resources. The response was that managers do not receive allocated budgets, and the practice is to submit requests for funds as needed. This led to selective funding approvals. Initially, it was relatively easy to secure funding when requested. Over time, however, the CDO's requests for crucial resources were often denied, suggesting that DEI was viewed as a secondary activity rather than a strategic priority. The president's actions made it clear that DEI was not considered a core aspect of the company's objectives. Priorities that the leadership valued received funding, while less valued initiatives, like DEI, did not.

Despite the limited support, the CDO used her training to implement basic changes. One example was in recruitment, where the hiring of a woman of East Indian background for a sales position led to an immediate boost in the company's profits in India. This success demonstrated the tangible benefits of cultural diversity and highlighted the missed opportunities resulting from the lack of broader investment in DEI. When DEI is treated as a charitable endeavor rather than a strategic necessity, it becomes vulnerable to being displaced by new priorities or budget cuts during economic downturns. When considered non-essential, DEI offices and initiatives are often among the first to face budget reductions. Organizations must embed DEI into their overall business strategy to achieve lasting impact, aligning it with their mission and objectives and providing financial support to ensure its success. Even well-trained practitioners cannot fully succeed without leadership commitment and resources, though too many unprepared practitioners are expected to do so.

DEI has often been framed primarily as a moral obligation and expected to address the pervasive social and institutional unfairness that has shaped society and the workplace from a charitable perspective. While this ethical foundation remains important, a purely moral lens limits

DEI's potential to transform organizations. To sustain and maximize the impact of DEI, leaders must also embrace its strategic value, particularly in an era of rapid globalization, heightened competition for talent, and the demands of a knowledge-sharing economy. The strategic advantage lens may be off-putting for those at the bottom of the organizational hierarchy, who have endured systemic injustice intergenerationally, as well as for social justice allies. They may view it as reducing people to commodities and ignoring the basic dignity they rightfully deserve.

Leaders have understandably struggled to balance the need for employees to feel valued with the need to remain competitive. The good news is that a creative coexistence approach integrates both perspectives into a business model that combines talent management, knowledge sharing, and equity from a mutually beneficial standpoint.

Talent Management, the Knowledge Economy, and Cultural Diversity, Equity, and Inclusion

The traditional talent management model that emphasizes hiring and retaining top talent based on qualifications and skills was effective in the manufacturing economy. Economic success then relied on mass production, cost efficiency, and tangible assets, with labor primarily involving manual work. Innovation, collaboration, and intellectual capital drive success in the current knowledge economy. Competitive advantage depends on leveraging research, technology, and culturally diverse expertise.

The talent pool and workforce demographics have also shifted, making DEI essential for effective talent management. Organizations that successfully attract the best and brightest without a strategy to harness the collective talent cannot take full advantage of it for knowledge sharing and teamwork. Cultural diversity becomes a liability rather than an asset. Equity, Cultural Diversity, & Inclusion Competency (ECDI) expertise is critical in addressing these challenges.

Integrating DEI into all stages of the employee lifecycle, from hiring to retirement, fosters long-term organizational success. Despite shifts in the labor market, a global talent shortage persists. Forbes and the Harvard Business Review highlight millions of unfilled positions, exacerbated by demographic changes (Harvard Business Publishing Corporate Learning, 2021; Quillian, L., Elo, I., Roksa, J., & Painter, M., 2023; Callaham, S., 2024, April 25). Today's workforce spans five generations, with increasing representation of women, nonbinary individuals, and underrepresented racial and ethnic groups. At the current growth rate, by 2030, Hispanics or Latinos will account for 78% of new workers, while H-1B visas continue to bring skilled talent from abroad. African Americans and Native Americans remain underutilized, collectively representing a labor pool that is under-recruited. Institutions have largely failed to prepare for these demographic shifts. A major reason for this failure is the lack of DEI expertise necessary to reimagine organizational culture and develop strategic action plans. Another factor is the current governmental attack on DEI within organizations.

Another factor changing the concept of talent is the shift from manufacturing to a knowledge economy, which has transformed how organizations manage talent. Knowledge is now a key economic asset, requiring businesses to emphasize collaboration, agility, and the sharing of information and expertise. Knowledge-sharing fosters innovation and efficiency, but cultural diversity can create miscommunication and power dynamics without equity and inclusion competency.

The global economy is increasingly shifting from reliance on manual labor to leveraging intellectual assets such as insights, skills, and experiences. This transformation, known as the knowledge-sharing economy, prioritizes exchanging expertise, collaboration, and innovation as key drivers of organizational success. Integrating DEI principles into the knowledge-sharing economy is essential to unlocking its full potential. Implementing DEI aligned with knowledge-sharing practices can foster creativity, improve decision-making, and boost productivity by empowering diverse teams and supporting organizational goals.

When DEI and knowledge-sharing principles are strategically aligned, the benefits extend across the organization:

- Enhanced Workforce Productivity: DEI-focused knowledge-sharing initiatives boost engagement, encouraging employees to contribute their unique insights, which enhances overall productivity.
- Employee Development: By integrating mentorship and training programs with DEI principles, organizations can create growth opportunities for HMEG employees and address inequities in professional development and career mobility.
- Talent Retention: Organizations that prioritize and embrace culturally diverse perspectives are more likely to retain top talent, as employees feel valued and appreciated.

Talent Needs to Be Managed to Exploit Knowledge-Sharing Fully

To fully leverage the benefits of knowledge sharing and the economy, organizations must actively address the challenges that cultural diversity poses. This new approach shifts how organizations harness intellectual assets for success, requiring businesses to create systems that encourage full participation in knowledge-sharing activities. Doing so enhances innovation and productivity, ensuring that all employees contribute to and benefit from the collective knowledge base. The integration of talent management, knowledge sharing, and managing cultural diversity holds great potential for next-generation DEI strategies.

In summary, organizations that embed DEI into talent management and knowledge-sharing strategies create cohesive teams, attract and retain top talent, and drive long-term success. When employees can share and build on each other's knowledge and expertise, companies become more agile, innovative, and capable of accumulating information quickly and efficiently. As globalization and demographic shifts reshape the workforce, effectively managing cultural diversity is no longer optional—it's a competitive necessity.

The modern workforce demands a new approach that requires fully integrating DEI principles into business operations. By embedding DEI throughout the employee lifecycle, businesses can foster a workplace culture that is equitable, inclusive, and poised for long-term success. Strategic DEI implementation ensures resilience in an evolving economic and political landscape while addressing historical inequities that hinder productivity. Organizations must prioritize the integration of DEI into operations to improve talent management and knowledge-sharing.

The Need for Leveling the Playing Field

The above assumes a need to redefine the relationships among team members and a direct report-manager relationship less defined by power relations. In a culturally diverse workplace, hierarchical relationships between managers and direct reports are strained by systemic inequities, power imbalances, and cultural misunderstandings. Removing these sources of misunderstandings and conflict fosters trust, engagement, and mutual respect, leading to a more effective and productive work environment. When inequities such as favoritism, bias in promotions, or lack of access to resources are removed, employees feel valued and motivated to contribute. Managers benefit from a more engaged workforce that is proactive, innovative, and aligned with organizational goals.

A workplace where workers have individual and team agency fosters autonomy, authority, and the ability to make decisions in their role, increasing organizational success. Management's role shifts from authoritarian oversight to being a source of encouragement, cooperativeness, and supportiveness. That involves removing barriers that hinder autonomy and self-reliance. Removing inequities fosters a two-way dialogue where direct reports feel empowered to share ideas, seek guidance, and provide constructive feedback. We describe how this works in our Managing for Equity in the Workplace training, and how developing the competency allows them to focus on higher-level responsibilities, including coaching and employee professional development.

A culture of transparency reduces misunderstandings, enabling managers to lead with greater clarity and effectiveness. When employees perceive fairness in opportunities for growth, promotion, and recognition, they are more likely to trust leaders, communicate openly, and offer feedback. In such environments, managers earn respect through competence rather than authority, and employees are more willing to follow leaders who demonstrate fairness, openness, and a commitment to DEI.

When equity is prioritized, the organization's hierarchy is seen not as a system of control but as a natural framework for decision-making, mentorship, and career development. By addressing inequities, organizations make hierarchical relationships more functional, respectful, and productive. This is particularly necessary in culturally diverse workplaces where fairness and inclusion are key to success.

Hierarchies are not inherently problematic. The challenge lies in ensuring they are equitable. Equitable hierarchical systems reduce conflict, power struggles, and perceptions of unfairness, creating space for meaningful engagement, especially among historically marginalized groups often positioned at lower organizational levels. In contrast, poorly designed DEI efforts can hinder collaboration and increase legal risks if not grounded in expertise. The mixed DEI to date indicates that organizations must reimagine their DEI approaches to build cultures where equity, inclusion, and systemic fairness are fully integrated and sustainable.

Chapter 4: Social Stratification & Organizational Change

A seasoned female transit operator took a new job in a nearby city and initially experienced a smooth transition. However, when the fare box on her bus malfunctioned before her shift, she sought help at the terminal. She approached two fellow operators who, based on their lower employee numbers, held seniority. Initially willing to help, their attitude shifted after noticing her higher ID number. Realizing she was a recent hire, they told her to figure it out on her own, as everyone else had. She felt demoralized and mistreated. This real-life example illustrates how workplace hierarchies can undermine collegiality and create unnecessary barriers to teamwork.

Perhaps the most crucial facet of American life that reproduces and maintains unfairness is how hierarchical relationships among different segments of society have unfolded since the founding of the United States. European colonists brought with them governance systems and social hierarchies that reflected the feudal and class-based structures of their home countries. In transplanting European governance structures, the colonists accepted the societal stratifications that contributed to fleeing their old country. These systems emphasized stratification based on land ownership, wealth, and titles, with power concentrated in the hands of the elite. Justifications for hierarchical segregation included ideologies related to property ownership, gender, race, and religion. The result is that a hierarchy was inherent in the founding of the United States.

From its beginning, the American Constitution was steeped in language and omissions that created entrenched hierarchies and systemic inequities. These historical inequities continue to shape the country's values and beliefs about the managing cultural differences among citizens today. This has had unfortunate consequences for meeting the needs of today's culturally diverse society. The Constitution's (1) compromise on slavery, (2) lack of detail about citizenship, (3) gender inequities, (4) exclusive property rights protections, (5) granting states the power to determine how citizens are treated, and (6) absence of language addressing equality and equity among America's historically marginalized and excluded groups continue to shape racial, ethnic, able-bodied differences, religion, sexual orientation, and gender equity. It includes provisions like the political compromise that counted enslaved individuals as three-fifths of a person for representation and taxation purposes, further dehumanizing both free and enslaved African Americans by institutionalizing their subjugation. As a result, the vestiges of racial and gender hierarchies enshrined in the nation's founding principles continue to shape racial group dynamics.

Similarly, the Fugitive Slave Clause, along with the lack of language abolishing slavery, prioritized historically majority and included group property rights over democratic rights. The Constitution left it to individual states to decide who was counted as citizens. Congress reserved the right to naturalize people, but this only applied to free historically majority and included group male immigrants' superior rights, thereby codifying a stratified hierarchy into law. Women did not have explicit guarantees of rights and freedoms. The Constitution excluded them from voting, holding office, and participating fully in civic life, reinforcing a hierarchy that prioritized historically majority and included group males' privileges and dominance in both public and private spheres.

Prioritizing property over democratic principles provided property ownership and land acquisition as rights and representation in ways that disproportionately benefited wealthy historically majority and included group landowners. Other shortcomings, such as the denial of land claims to Indigenous peoples and the lack of legal claims to property ownership for enslaved individuals, contribute to lagging equity along racial and gender lines. Prioritizing property over personhood reinforced economic hierarchies tied to race, gender, and class. The Constitution allowed local governments to maintain and enforce discriminatory practices, including segregation, institutionalized inequities, and barriers to individual and group economic mobility. This patchwork governance structure resulted in the perpetuation of systemic inequities, particularly in regions of the country with a history of slavery and colonization.

The founders' shortcomings resulted in a document that lacked explicit language guaranteeing equity, protection against oppression, or specific measures to address systemic discrimination. As a result, the country continues to grapple with expanding rights through organized protests and legal battles. The Constitution's omissions allowed inequitable systems to persist, as the framers primarily focused on protecting the interests of their dominant class of historically majority and included group males. Over time, social and economic stratification has spurred historically marginalized and excluded American citizens to mobilize for social and economic justice. The civil rights movement of the mid-20th century initiated some of the most transformative changes in United States history concerning citizen rights due to mostly Black bodies mobilizing and taking to the streets to demand justice and fairness. They demanded dismantling legal segregation, addressing systemic racial discrimination, and broadening protections for marginalized groups. Their leaders, such as Martin Luther King, Jr. and Malcolm X, were labeled communists for their progressive civil rights activism and fight for economic justice. The advocacy for systemic change, including desegregation, economic equity, and the dismantling of institutional racism, was intended to dismantle the hierarchy along racial lines.

In summary, the Constitution established systems of privilege and exclusion that served the interests of the historically powerful majority and included group members. The vestiges of the legally sanctioned inequities persist, especially as the country becomes culturally diverse. Disparities in wealth, education, housing, and representation reflect these historical hierarchies. Systemic racism, gender inequality, and debates over immigration and Indigenous rights trace their roots to the Constitution's original framework. Efforts to address these inequities through amendments, legislation, and social movements are ongoing, but the founding principles and omissions remain. That is what makes it challenging to attenuate the hierarchies. As the country's cultural diversity increases, inconsistencies in the values Americans espouse and the rules of law we uphold are called into question.

Social Stratification and Historical Resistance to DEI

Most modern organizations and workplaces continue to adopt hierarchical structures for operational efficiency. There is nothing inherently problematic about hierarchies in the workplace. The lines of authority are clear, roles are defined, and responsibilities are clarified. Trouble arises when a historically majority and included group, a male-dominated workplace, becomes culturally diverse without diversity management efforts. You can predict where the average person likely falls on both the societal and workplace hierarchies based on their race and gender. The result is that all too often, even if a historically marginalized and excluded group member has equal or better qualifications, a historically majority and included group member is more likely to receive the job or promotion. A study by Bertrand and Mullainathan (2004) found that resumes with applicant names stereotyped as belonging to an historically majority and included group received 50% more callbacks for interviews than identical resumes with stereotypically African American-sounding names, highlighting significant racial bias in hiring decisions (Quillian, L., Elo, I., Roksa, J., & Painter, M., 2023). Women of historically marginalized and excluded groups are also more likely to experience inequity in the workplace in terms of pay, mobility, and qualifications.

In most cases, it would be a mistake to imagine the top leaders sitting in a backroom behind closed doors, orchestrating ways to create and maintain a hierarchy that favors them. That's not necessary. All that is needed is to increase cultural diversity in a hierarchical workplace by hiring a culturally diverse workforce without consciously creating equity. The organizational hierarchy will soon reflect the racial and gender segmentation witnessed in the larger society.

Cultural diversity disrupts traditional hierarchies, necessitating effective talent management. Differences in cultural norms, problem-solving styles, and communication can create misunderstandings, stereotypes about performance and cultural fit, and perceptions of unfairness within hierarchical organizations. Even when implementing cultural diversity management practices, practitioners often rely on DEI initiatives, programs, and best practices that fail to effectively address the deep-rooted inequities that undermine productivity and increase legal jeopardy. Managers rely on trial-and-error diversity best practices when organizational culture change strategies are not deployed. That leads to inefficiencies and resistance. DEI efforts fail due to a lack of understanding of the barriers to equity and reliance on surface-level solutions, resulting in inefficiencies, resistance, and legal risks.

In summary, organizational culture change is essential for creating inclusive, equitable, and culturally diverse workplaces that run smoothly. By addressing the systemic barriers and leveraging the strengths of cultural diversity, organizations can foster environments where all employees feel valued and supported. Such transformations are needed to enhance employee well-being and efficient and effective knowledge sharing for sustained productivity. This requires understanding how the existing culture stifles inclusion, creates unnecessary obstacles, and harms teamwork.

The Role of Hierarchies in Workforce Stratification

There is nothing inherently inequitable about hierarchical organizations. Communication and decision-making frequently follow a top-down approach in such structures. A hierarchical organization functions best when it successfully integrates efficiency, accountability, adaptability, and equity into its framework. However, significant challenges arise as the workforce becomes increasingly culturally diverse, especially if a cultural diversity management plan has not been implemented. These challenges arise due to communication barriers, differing work norms, and conflicts in decision-making styles.

Team members perform better when there is clear communication and streamlined processes. Cultural differences can create communication barriers due to variations in language proficiency, accents, and communication styles (e.g., indirect vs. direct). Some cultures emphasize punctuality and deadlines, while others have a more flexible approach to time and schedules. This can lead to frustrations in project coordination, especially when those with a high need for punctuality encounter team members who prioritize taking the time to complete their work proficiently, even if it takes longer. Differences also exist in how cultures approach accountability, with some emphasizing individual responsibility and others prioritizing collective effort. This difference can create ambiguity regarding task ownership. For instance, a highly valued Japanese team member who is recognized individually for a team achievement may feel discomfort at being the sole recipient of credit, as it can undermine the team's unity and cause the employee to lose face if their colleagues aren't also acknowledged.

Other cultural differences that can impact workplace efficiency and productivity include feedback and conflict resolution styles, comfort in challenging leadership decisions, management style expectations, gender differences and identities, socioeconomic class differences, and religion. These differences must be managed effectively to meet both workforce and organizational needs while ensuring efficiency and productivity. One of the most crucial considerations for managing cultural diversity is reducing the impact of hierarchical systems that lead to inequitable outcomes.

A hierarchical system limits input from lower-level employees, where most historically marginalized group members are overrepresented. This results in a sense of marginalization that compounds personal experiences of exclusion. Furthermore, hierarchical structures perpetuate microinequities, unequal resource allocation, and biased performance evaluations, negatively affecting job satisfaction and engagement. When historically majority and included group members are overrepresented at the top and historically marginalized people at the bottom, inequity worsens. The result is that talent in the organization is hindered if not suffocated.

Positions historically marginalized and excluded group employees are likely to fill have lower job security, leading to increased volatility. They face a greater likelihood of layoffs, exposure to safety risks (e.g., accidents, assaults), and public scrutiny. Budget cuts and automation (e.g., automated ticketing and driverless vehicles) threaten their employment. Additionally, they experience higher stress and burnout due to long hours, dealing with difficult customers, physically demanding work, and often unpredictable schedules. One avenue they seek to overcome these challenges is upward mobility within the organization. However, there are too often few promotion pathways available to them. Despite years of experience, many struggle to enter management due to inequitable hiring and promotion practices. They have too few allies in management and executive levels and seldom feel heard or seen by those in power.

Leadership opportunities often favor internal networks or outsiders with college degrees, leaving out frontline BIPOC employees. Requirements for management often include degrees or certifications that frontline workers may not have access to. They are seldom included in key decisions

Billy E. Vaughn

that affect them (e.g., scheduling, safety measures, wages) or allowed to contribute their wisdom to solving pressing problems. These factors contribute to a sense of hopelessness among this essential segment of the workforce, which the organization relies on to fulfill its mission.

There is no need to imagine a group of leaders meeting secretly in the organization to maintain a hierarchy that benefits them. They don't have to. All that is needed is a culturally diverse workforce without a commitment to cultural diversity management. The color-coded hierarchy will emerge naturally. One of the primary troublemakers contributing to inequities is bias.

Social psychology research shows that inequities in hierarchical organizations result from actions that undermine fairness, such as hiring and promoting people within our social circle and showing bias against those perceived as not belonging. Biases that justify a color-coded hierarchy are especially harmful, even when unconscious. Social dominance orientation (SDO) theory offers insights into how bias supports and maintains hierarchical systems even when decision-makers are aware of the inequities (Pratto, F., Sidanius, J., & Levin, S., 2006).

Types of Social Dominance Orientation

Social Dominance Orientation (SDO) is a personality trait that reflects an individual's preference for a socioeconomic hierarchy in which certain groups have higher status and more relational power than others. This partly explains how group-based hierarchies are maintained through institutionalized unfairness, individual biases, and ideological support systems. As a psychological construct, SDO measures an individual's inclination for hierarchy and dominance in social settings, offering insights into attitudes towards DEI. Research has identified a continuum of SDO levels, each associated with distinct values and beliefs that shape an individual's DEI perspective:

92

High SDOs (Hierarchy Enhancers) individuals support hierarchies that stratify people. They view stratification as natural and desirable and oppose DEI's aim to address this imbalance. High SDO individuals actively design, develop, and maintain institutional policies, leadership behaviors, and workplace norms that systematically reproduce inequities in several ways.

1. Individuals high in SDO tend to seek leadership positions where they can reinforce existing power imbalances. They surround themselves with those who share their views and work with them to increase their status and gain power over the organization.

2. They frame DEI initiatives as threats to meritocracy rather than solutions that foster productivity and reduce systemic disparities affecting the general workforce.

3. They emphasize hiring and promoting individuals based on "cultural fit" rather than skills, often excluding the historically marginalized from leadership pipelines and reinforcing historically majority leadership structures.

4. They support a discriminatory culture by promoting competition over collaboration, supporting exclusionary practices, and normalizing microinequities, leaving the historically marginalized vulnerable.

5. When an HMIG hires an historically marginalized, they are often relegated to a symbolic role, such as staffing the front desk to greet visitors, instead of being assigned a more substantial contributor role, even when they are qualified. Job positions available to them offer limited upward mobility.

6. High SDO leaders frequently justify racial, and gender pay gaps by attributing salary disparities to "performance," rationalizing away rather than acknowledging the structural inequities the historically marginalized face.

7. High SDOs in decision-making positions tend to offer promotions to those who conform to dominant cultural norms, disproportionately disadvantaging historically marginalized and excluded groups.

8. Biased hiring and performance evaluations, driven by stereotypes and implicit bias, ensure that top positions remain predominantly filled by historically majority males.

9. High SDO individuals actively resist DEI policies and practices, such as affirmative action, pay equity laws, or inclusive hiring practices, viewing them as unfair practices that undermine merit and individual contributions.

10. The reinforcement of workplace hierarchies under SDO leadership contributes to increased psychological stress, disengagement, and a decline in well-being among the historically marginalized.

High SDO individuals pursue leadership roles to maintain existing power structures and oppose DEI initiatives, viewing them as threats to meritocracy. They prioritize "cultural fit" over qualifications and exclude historically marginalized and excluded groups from leadership pipelines, even when they are better qualified.

Moderate-High SDOs (Passive Reinforcers) accept the existing hierarchy but do not actively seek to enhance existing inequities. They are indifferent to DEI practices and policies aimed at reducing inequity.

Moderate SDOs (Ambivalent Pragmatists) recognize and acknowledge disparities. They support equality (which they do not differentiate from equity) in principle but may lack commitment to specific actions or policies that promote it.

Moderate-Low SDO (Reluctant Reformers) views hierarchies as problematic and supports efforts to reduce them. They engage in or endorse initiatives aimed at promoting equality and equity, though they may approach these efforts cautiously and incrementally.

Low SDOs (Hierarchy Attenuators). strongly oppose social hierarchies, viewing them as unjust and unfair. They actively support DEI policies and work toward dismantling systemic inequities. Low SDOs are more likely to be social justice advocates.

SDO plays a significant role in shaping attitudes toward DEI. High-SDO individuals actively reinforce hierarchies, especially in leadership roles, and resist DEI efforts and policies that maintain existing power structures. Moderate-High SDOs are aware of inequities but do not actively challenge or change them. Moderate SDOs recognize disparities but lack the commitment to addressing them. Moderate-Low SDOs support equity efforts cautiously, whereas Low-SDO individuals are the strongest advocates for dismantling systemic inequities and promoting inclusive workplace policies.

The SDO categories illustrate the spectrum of attitudes and behaviors related to social dominance and hierarchy. Understanding where individuals fall on this continuum can help inform strategies for anticipating resistance, fostering inclusive leadership, and effectively implementing DEI initiatives.

The Need for Organizational Culture Change

Most organizations operate within hierarchical structures where authority and decision-making flow from top to bottom. While this system provides operational and decision-making clarity and control, it reinforces power dynamics, biases, and barriers to equity and inclusion. For example, historically marginalized and excluded group employees often encounter pay inequity and limited career advancement opportunities due to traditional decision-making methods that may undermine fairness, either by design or inadvertently. These inequities frequently contradict the organization's espoused DEI values regarding talent. Leadership is often unaware of these inequities and the lack of alignment, making it difficult for them to accept and act when unfairness is pointed out, even by the DEI leader.

The Chief People Officer informed Salesforce CEO Marc Benioff about gender pay inequity within the company. Initially, he was skeptical and did not believe pay disparities existed at Salesforce, as he considered the company a champion of equality. The Chief People Officer and her team requested permission to collect data to show that women at Salesforce were paid less than their male counterparts for similar work. Despite his skepticism, Benioff agreed to a company-wide pay audit. The results confirmed a significant pay gap, prompting Salesforce to allocate $3 million to address these disparities. The following year, another audit revealed additional gaps due to acquisitions and workforce changes, leading to another round of salary adjustments.

Benioff later became a vocal advocate for pay equity, acknowledging his initial reluctance and emphasizing the importance of data-driven decision-making in confronting workplace inequities. His journey from skepticism rooted in egalitarian ideals to championing equity highlights the challenges leaders and management face in recognizing and addressing systemic barriers to equity. This real-life example of efforts to promote equity within an organization also illustrates the limitations of an equality-focused approach to DEI. Even when fair practices are believed to be in place, there is no guarantee unless data are collected to back it up. Achieving equity requires understanding how hierarchical systems can inadvertently create inequities without active efforts to uncover the policies and practices that lead to unfairness.

Organizational Structures That Reduce the Impact of Hierarchies

The lack of inclusion in hierarchical organizations has led companies, particularly startups that rely on younger generations of workers, to seek alternative structures. In contrast to a hierarchy, a flat or horizontally structured organization minimizes stratified roles and responsibilities by valuing employees regardless of their title and position, emphasizing collaborative or team decision-making. Companies like Zappos, Valve Corporation, and Spotify exemplify this approach, which fosters innovation and agility. By decentralizing authority, flat organizations create environments where diverse perspectives are valued, and all employees feel included. This primarily makes historically marginalized and excluded groups feel included and appreciated. The organizations are more likely to have a cultural diversity program, and rely on principles of self-governing teams, building a culture of trust, and referring to everyone as a team member or associate regardless of position. The leadership is likely to have a Moderate to Moderate-Low SDO, which results in a tenuous commitment to DEI that is easily affected by resistance or backlash.

The relationship between a hierarchically structured workplace and how much workers feel included is influenced by various factors, including representation, communication, power dynamics, and bias. It is essential for organizations to actively work toward creating an inclusive and equitable work environment that values cultural diversity and provides opportunities for all employees to grow professionally. Organizational culture significantly affects how much workers feel included in a hierarchically structured workplace. The leadership's SDO personality determines the extent to which inequities will be reinforced. Historically marginalized and excluded groups are more sensitive to hierarchies, especially when relegated as a group to the bottom organizational strata. This is especially true for African American workers due to a racial history of exclusion and subjugation. A culture that incorporates DEI creates an environment where all employees feel respected, valued, and supported, and everyone has an equal chance of actualizing their potential.

Flat or horizontal companies rely on transparency, employee autonomy, and collaborative team structures rather than rigid hierarchies, fostering innovation and agility in decision-making. Few levels of management between staff and executives characterize a horizontal structure. In these organizations, employees often have more responsibility and autonomy than their counterparts in hierarchical structures. Many technology startups and modern companies have adopted flat organizational structures to foster better communication, collaboration, innovation, and agility. In these structures, there's minimal hierarchy and a stronger emphasis on self-management (Vaara, E., Harju, A., Leppälä, M. & Buffart, M., 2021).

Several well-known organizations have started out with intentional flat organizational structures, only to include hierarchical features after the organization grows. These include:

- **Valve Corporation:** This video game developer is known for creating flat, self-organizing teams that lack formal hierarchies and job titles. Employees choose projects they're passionate about and have a high degree of autonomy. It maintains flatness today, but acknowledges informal hierarchies and coordination challenges. Valve remains one of the most profitable and innovative gaming companies. However, struggles to scale and coordinate large projects (Macgregor, J. (2023, January 27).

- **Zappos:** The online shoe retailer has adopted a version of a flat structure called "Holacracy," which did not have managers in an effort to distribute authority and leadership throughout the organization. Zappos transitioned to a more hierarchical, market-based organization to better clarify roles and increase accountability (Rajan, A., 2016, January 14).

- **Spotify:** The music streaming company organizes its employees into autonomous "squads," "chapters," and "guilds," providing each with a degree of independence while ensuring successful alignment with the company's goals. The company later introduced formal leadership roles for strategic alignment while retaining team autonomy (Spotify, 2023, January 23).

Practical DEI goals involve establishing an organization where leaders at the top of the pyramid feel accountable for balancing the organization's objectives with the equity needs of its workforce. Hierarchies are not the problem. It is the way in which cultural diversity in the workplace is managed that matters. While hierarchies serve an important structure for productivity, finding ways to reduce inequities is the key to reducing the inequities inherent in them. More work needs to be done to find the best models and practices for creating flat organizations as these real world experiments indicate.

The Necessity for Shifting to an Equitable Culture

The shift toward an equitable culture in hierarchical organizations is crucial for several reasons. First, by serving workforce needs, the organization reflects the principles of inclusion, equity, and valuing cultural diversity. By catering to a broader range of workers, organizations can leverage their increased engagement and ensure that their products, services, and policies are accessible and beneficial to a larger segment of customers. This focus also helps businesses tap into new markets and diverse customer segments.

Shifting to a stronger emphasis on serving the workforce's needs allows organizations to address systemic inequities that currently favor the dominant, smaller-in-size group at the top levels of the pyramid. Many organizations have historically been structured around the needs and preferences of the privileged few, neglecting the equity needs of marginalized or underrepresented groups. Consider the public transportation sector in large metropolitan areas. Black, brown, and Asian workers tend to be overrepresented in public-facing jobs and volatile job roles that compromise their safety at work, such as bus drivers. Bus drivers and parking enforcement workers are examples. In one transit agency with an overall historically majority and included group representation of 15%, they represent one 100% at the executive level. None of these leaders have direct experience in low-level job roles. Historically marginalized and excluded groups make up the lower-level jobs.

This lack of cultural diversity among decision-makers has sometimes resulted in poor safety decisions due to not taking workers' complaints about their safety seriously and implementing transportation route designs that undermine the needs of marginalized communities that rely the most on public transportation (Attoh, K. A., 2019). Not surprisingly, the transportation needs of middle-class commuters traveling from the suburbs into the inner city tend to overshadow those of the public living in and more frequently utilizing it within the main transportation coverage areas, thereby reproducing the hierarchy in the public sector.

By actively working toward serving the masses, especially those most in need of public services, organizations can contribute to dismantling inequities and creating both a more successful organization and a just and fair society. Additionally, embracing organizational change that prioritizes serving the workforce as a whole is essential for the long-term viability and sustainability of the business. As societal expectations and demographics change, organizations that fail to adapt become irrelevant or even face abandonment from consumers and stakeholders. Flat organizations make everyone feel included, especially historically marginalized and excluded group members, who often have the lowest sense of belonging in hierarchical, majority-white male organizations. Organizations that aim to increase an equitable environment must emphasize culture change.

When strategically implemented, organizational change is essential for creating inclusive, culturally diverse, and equitable organizations. The process involves deliberate shifts in an organization's culture to address the structures and processes that reinforce existing inequities. It creates an equitable environment where all employees are valued and appreciated, fostering growth and success. But what is organizational culture?

Chapter 5: Organizational Culture & Change

Organizational culture encapsulates the shared values, beliefs, and practices that define how members interact with one another, make decisions, and engage with the world. From how leadership communicates to the unspoken rules governing workplace behavior, culture profoundly influences an organization's success or failure.

This section explores culture's critical role in shaping an organization's dynamics, effectiveness, and ability to adapt. Culture is not static. It evolves through leadership vision, employee behavior, and external influences. Examples include hiring a new leader based on their vision to improve the organization, employees demanding that the organization change policies to support social justice, and changes in the legal landscape demanding changes in business practices.

Organizational culture is an organization's personality. It expresses the core values shared throughout the organization. Culture is captured in the organization's mission, values, and vision and shapes behaviors that drive decisions, relationships, and activities. It is determined and bolstered by its members' shared beliefs and practices. Culture underlies decision-making and problem-solving processes individually and in teams.

Organizational culture has been defined in different ways over time, and it can encompass a broad range of factors, including the organizational structure, leadership style, policies, and success philosophy. For our purposes, organizational culture refers to the shared values, beliefs, values, taboos, and practices that shape the behaviors of individual members of an organization. Culture influences how an organization's structure and employees interact with each other and with customers. It encompasses a variety of elements, including work environment, company mission, values, ethics, expectations, and goals. It is vital for the success of an organization since it helps to unify and motivate employees. Creating and maintaining an effective organizational culture is essential for achieving business goals. Communication, collaboration, creativity, openness, and trust all create a solid organizational culture.

Organizational development and organizational effectiveness are crucial to culture change. Organizational development is a planned effort to increase an organization's effectiveness and efficiency, often involving interventions to improve an organization's processes, structures, or strategies. In practice, it consists of improving and evolving the organization to meet its goals better. An example is implementing a DEI-focused leadership development program. A company recognizes the business benefits of having a culturally diverse leadership team, but currently has an all-historically majority and included group male team. A DEI-focused leadership development program is launched that includes mentorship, sponsorship, and targeted training for high-potential historically marginalized and excluded group employees. The goal is to increase the pipeline of diverse leaders and equip the historically majority group managers with inclusive leadership skills.

The relationship between organizational culture and organizational development is closely intertwined. Through organizational development, an organization can understand the needs of its employees, define clear standards and expectations, and create an atmosphere that encourages engagement and innovation. Organizational development starts with assessing the organizational culture, which is pivotal for successfully implementing development strategies. A well-aligned culture fosters positive changes, facilitates the adoption of new practices, and makes the organization more agile and responsive to market demands.

Moreover, organizational development efforts can foster a positive culture among organization members, creating environments where employees are motivated, engaged, and productive. Initiatives designed to modify or transform the organizational culture must align with the organization's goals and objectives. Thus, the synergy between organizational culture and development is essential in steering the organization toward sustainable growth and success. It ensures that the organization evolves cohesively and harmoniously, promoting adaptability and resilience in a competitive market.

Organizational effectiveness refers to an organization's ability to achieve its mission, meet its strategic goals, and maximize performance while fostering an inclusive, equitable, and diverse workplace culture. From an ECDI perspective, organizational effectiveness is measured by how well an organization integrates equity fairness in its structures, policies, practices, and decision-making processes to drive sustainable success.

IEC is also a key component of organizational effectiveness. An organization committed to creating a culturally diverse, equitable, and inclusive environment can maximize employee potential and best serve its customer base. This environment increases understanding and acceptance, promotes fairness, and ensures the organization's competitiveness. A workplace that implements inclusion initiatives to provide an engaging, open, and supportive environment is best positioned to increase productivity. An equitable culture is key to an effective, culturally diverse organization.

Organizational culture determines success or failure. Members rely on understanding and conforming to the shared norms and values to behave within the boundaries and avoid taboo behavior (i.e., behavior that is considered outside the boundaries). Changing an organization's culture when necessary is the key to adjusting to turbulence in an effort to remain competitive. Creating an equitable culture to harness cultural diversity in the service of productivity is the key to the ECDI change framework.

In summary, culture affects everything from employee engagement and retention to innovation and organizational reputation. To reduce the impact of hierarchical relationships in a culturally diverse workplace, changing the culture to put equity at the center is the key to sustaining competitiveness. Understanding how culture develops and evolves is key to fostering an environment that supports inclusion, equity, and growth.

Changing Organizational Culture as the Foundation for ECDI Work

At its best, ECDI initiatives aim to transform a culture of inequity and exclusion into an environment in which everyone, from entry-level staff to top leadership, perceives that they can thrive. Achieving culture change is no small feat. Organizational culture often reinforces established norms and practices that resist transformation. This resistance is particularly evident in organizations striving to address systemic inequities or implement racial equity mandates. Despite well-intentioned initiatives, deeply ingrained habits and unspoken rules frequently undermine progress, requiring deliberate efforts to realign culture with organizational values. Culture is deeply rooted in history, habits, and power structures, making it resistant to rapid transformation. People naturally gravitate toward familiar practices, and organizational systems often perpetuate the status quo, even when they no longer effectively serve the organization's goals.

Disagreements about the culture change goal can stagnate change. Even if an ECDI leader can effectively help the top leadership see the value in using an equity lens to drive change, the middle management may not agree. Many will view it as "watering down talent" or reverse discrimination. This pushback signals to the ECDI practitioner that more preparation is needed to onboard the middle management before forging ahead, even with the top leader's endorsement. Efforts to implement equity-driven changes often falter due to insufficient accountability, resistance from middle management, or the emotional and practical challenges of disrupting established norms. These are examples of what makes changing organizational culture one of the most challenging aspects of ECDI work.

How Organizational Culture Evolves

Despite these challenges, an inequitable culture is a powerful lever for change. Organizations that successfully align their culture with stated goals demonstrate resilience, adaptability, and innovation. A well-cultivated culture fosters trust, collaboration, and a sense of belonging, empowering employees to perform at their best. By examining the elements and dynamics of culture, this section emphasizes how intentional culture change can drive equity and inclusion. It highlights the importance of leadership commitment, employee engagement, and sustained effort in creating an environment where everyone can thrive. As we delve deeper into the complexities of organizational culture, we'll uncover practical strategies for fostering transformation, addressing resistance, and building a culture that supports individual and organizational success. This journey begins with recognizing the fundamental role culture plays in shaping the future of work.

Leadership commitment, employee behavior, and external factors influence culture change. Understanding how organizational culture is created helps leaders intentionally design and foster a culture that aligns with organizational goals and values. Key factors that contribute to creating an organization's culture include (1) founders' vision, (2) leadership, (3) core values, (4) hiring practices, (5) communication structure, (6) rituals, symbols, and traditions, (7) policies and procedures, and (8) employee behavior and peer influence. The culture determines employee engagement, the organization's brand for attracting talent, and its innovation, collaboration, and adaptability, which are crucial for long-term success.

An organization's founders' values, beliefs, vision, and business philosophy serve as the foundation for the subsequent culture. Core values are the organization's cultural DNA that guides decisions and practices. They are also codified in value statements, employee handbooks, and policies. The leader plays a pivotal role in shaping the organization's culture by setting the tone for the workforce regarding what it means to embody the vision's values, beliefs, and behavior. The leader at the top may come and go. Once the culture is well-established, the middle management becomes the culture gatekeeper. No matter how charismatic a newly appointed leader is, they must influence their management team to get much done.

An organization's internal and external communication practices also shape its culture. The communication style determines transparency, collaboration, and recognition practices, which contribute to shaping the culture. Rituals, such as team meetings, celebrations, and awards, build a sense of shared identity. Office design, branding, and dress codes are symbols that influence how employees perceive and interact within the culture. These sources of information must be taken into consideration to uncover equity barriers.

Formal systems, including performance management, decision-making frameworks, and conflict resolution processes, establish expectations about how to behave within cultural boundaries. Taboo behaviors are seldom in formal documents. Newcomers tend to learn them through trial and error. Discovering on the first day that wearing business attire is considered overdressing in the organization is an example. ECDI policies, such as flexibility and work-life balance, reflect cultural priorities. Employees collectively contribute to organizational culture. Their actions, interactions, and attitudes reinforce norms and shared values. If they feel treated equitably, this increases commitment to the organization.

Organizational culture is not static. It evolves over time as it grows, faces new challenges, or undergoes leadership changes. Transformations such as mergers, technological advancements, new initiatives, and shifts in talent management due to employee demographic changes can reshape culture over time. By understanding the components and dynamics of organizational culture, leaders can take deliberate steps to create an environment that supports their organizational objectives and values.

What is Organizational Culture Change?

Organizational culture change is a complex and gradual shift from deeply ingrained values, behaviors, and norms to align with new priorities, goals, or external demands. Organizational culture is so deeply rooted that changing it requires a considerable amount of commitment, time, effort, and resources. That is why intentional change requires a strategic and structured process with clear goals and involves collaboration at all levels. Below is a set of phases commonly associated with organizational culture transformation. The key phases include:

1. Awareness Phase (A Business Imperative Arises): This phase involves recognizing the need for change.

2. Preparation Phase: Creating a plan, including a strategy for change, takes place in this phase.

3. Implementation Phase: This phase involves executing the change plan.

4. Transition Phase: Support for adaptation to the change is provided in this phase.

5. Consolidation Phase: This phase involves doing what is necessary to ensure the change is sustained.

6. Institutionalization Phase: This phase involves embedding the change into the organization's culture.

Completing the change process steps transforms an organization's culture through a strategic and structured approach that requires commitment, clear goals, and collaboration. Each phase builds on the previous one, ensuring a systematic method for lasting cultural transformation and incorporating the change into the organization's culture for long-term adoption.

Changing an Organization's Culture Is Difficult

Organizational change is complicated for several reasons. One reason is that change involves a significant shift in an organization's culture or restructuring the way it carries out its mission. That change can be challenging for both employees and management. People are creatures of habit and often resist change because it is disruptive. The second reason is that change can be emotional, with some employees fearing the unfamiliar and resisting the unknown. Change requires management to focus on practical matters, such as implementing a new process, which is a third reason it is difficult. Practitioners often fail to consider the hidden aspects of culture, such as unspoken rules and practices, that have maintained the status quo. The result is inconsistent communication about why change is essential, the roadmap for creating change, and individual responsibilities and accountability.

An example is the challenges that arise after implementing a racial equity mandate. Despite initiative-driven changes in professional development policies and procedures designed to promote equity, management may unconsciously continue to promote individuals culturally similar to them. This undermines carrying out the mandate and increases a sense that the organization is not serious about changing. The NFL implemented the Rooney Rule in 2003, which requires teams to interview at least one BIPOC candidate for head coaching and senior football operations positions. The rule aimed to increase racial diversity in leadership roles within the league. The initial progress was good, but the efforts quickly began to falter. The number of BIPOC coaches rose from two in 2003 to seven in 2006. As of early 2025, only four of the thirty-two head coaches are Black, despite over 70% of NFL players being Black.

The Rooney Rule failed due to a lack of enforcement and accountability. The initiative suffered from checkbox interviews, resulting in limited conversions to hires and backsliding by the management.

Its parameters allowed decision-makers to circumvent its intentions without consequences. They often conducted perfunctory interviews with African American candidates to satisfy the rule without broad intentional efforts to hire the candidates. Leaving it up to decision-makers to "do the right thing" without oversight is a recipe for maintaining the status quo. The failure of the NFL's Rooney Rule to become standard practice illustrates this struggle: despite its intent to increase diversity in leadership, entrenched biases and systemic barriers have limited its effectiveness, highlighting the difficulty of achieving meaningful cultural change without strategies for reducing resistance, training the desired competencies, and enforcement.

The majority of the historically majority and included group ownership and executive ranks of the NFL resisted meaningful change, maintaining entrenched biases and preference for candidates that share their race and culture. There is a limited pipeline of BIPOC candidates in key feeder positions like offensive coordinator roles, which are often prerequisites for head coaching jobs, and statistical evidence indicates systemic discrimination, with historically majority and included group candidates being significantly more likely to be hired for those positions than their equally qualified historically marginalized and excluded group peers. Overall, the limited success of the Rooney Rule is attributed to cultural resistance and systemic biases that persist within the NFL's hiring practices. The result is that a sense of unfairness continues among racially marginalized sports coaches seeking entrance into elite positions and the majority of Black players at the bottom of the decision-making chain, hoping for change.

An additional reason organizational change can be challenging is that change requires years of sustained effort. Change is not a sprint. It's about getting to the finish line of a marathon. Change is, of course, possible, even when it requires significant effort and emotional support for those affected. Still, it is always challenging. It requires the right strategies, mindset, and quite a bit of compassion to overcome the challenges and stay the course. Listening to employees to learn about their fears and needs is a key strategy to make organizational change less difficult. Deeply listening to and addressing their concerns whenever possible will make their journey easier. It is also important to remember that everyone in the organization is going through change. Learning about their concerns, acknowledging them, and asking what can be done to address them quicker and positively help reduce fear of the unknown. Trust, support, and sustained engagement are thus the critical and much-needed factors for successful change.

For forward-thinking organizations that desire to become equitable successfully, the challenges of onboarding leadership, middle management, and the workforce increase considerably. Organizational change is difficult for many reasons, including emotional and practical challenges. Recognizing these challenges and taking critical steps to address them makes it possible to navigate change. An expert ECDI practitioner at the helm with resources and leverage in the organization is the key to success.

The Case for an Organizational Change Approach to DEI

DEI BPs are widely recognized solutions for promoting inclusion, increasing cultural diversity, and tackling immediate related challenges. DEI practitioners describe their work as transformative. However, few can articulate a formal culture change framework or model that guides their efforts. Many tend to list the DEI BPs that their organization has implemented. DEI BPs, such as diversity recruitment practices, are tactical, focusing on narrow areas of improvement rather than driving systemic change. They often adhere to standardized methods that are replicated across industries with minimal customization, relying on anecdotal success stories and limited data instead of considering an organization's unique dynamics. For instance, the typical diversity recruitment solution is not integrated into an organization-wide strategy or organizational culture change plan. Consequently, organizations experience a revolving door of diverse candidates who depart at rates that prevent reaching stated recruitment goals. The impact of DEI BPs is often limited to the specific area in which they are applied, leaving deeper cultural and systemic challenges unaddressed.

Transforming organizational culture requires a deliberate and comprehensive strategy based on equity-centered principles deeply embedded into every facet of an organization. An ECDI organizational change strategy has the following characteristics:

1. Scope: Focuses on broad, systemic transformation rather than isolated improvements.

2. Purpose: Aligns with the organization's mission, vision, and long-term goals, ensuring that equity-centered principles and solutions are embedded in the organizational DNA.

3. Customization: This process considers the organization's history, culture, and unique current challenges to create a tailored roadmap for change.

4. Impact: Designed to influence all aspects of the organization, from leadership accountability and employee behavior to operational processes and customer engagement.

5. Sustainability requires long-term commitment, continuous measurement, and the ability to adjust to new challenges and opportunities rapidly.

6. Outcome: The goal is to create an organization in which all levels of the organization have a voice, feel heard, experience equity, and optimally support organizational success.

The Equity, Cultural Diversity, & Inclusion Competency approach is a robust organizational change strategy that addresses root causes, reshapes cultural norms, and ensures alignment between operations and strategic objectives. It transforms DEI from a peripheral initiative into a central component of organizational success.

Lessons from Leading and Lagging Organizations

Organizations like Cisco, Novartis, and Mastercard have shown that the sustainability of DEI implementation improves when it is more deeply embedded in everyday operations. These companies have maintained their programs for at least fifteen years, even in the face of backlash. In contrast, others like Meta and Walmart have scaled back or abandoned their DEI commitments, highlighting the vulnerability of initiatives that lack strong leadership commitment and integration.

Walmart bolstered its DEI efforts after facing negative publicity and a prolonged gender pay inequity lawsuit. Its recent reduction of initiatives in response to external pressures suggests that DEI was not well integrated into the company's values. Meta initially embraced DEI initiatives to keep pace with broader corporate trends driven by political and legal shifts but reversed these efforts in early 2025. They are not alone. The post-George Floyd surge in DEI efforts and the ease with which these efforts were curtailed revealed the fragility of surface-level commitments.

A robust ECDI strategy must also account for legal risks. Even the most thoughtfully designed initiatives are susceptible to legal challenges without an integrated risk management plan. Organizations must navigate a climate of increasing backlash and skepticism toward DEI programs by balancing bold cultural transformation with risk mitigation. Organizations must prioritize systemic change with equity in the center to create an inclusive and equitable culture. This involves embedding ECDI principles into all aspects of operations, from leadership and policies to daily employee experiences. Key components include:

1. Ensuring ECDI efforts align with the organization's mission, vision, and values.

2. Moving beyond isolated initiatives to embed ECDI into every facet of the organization.

3. Establishing mechanisms to support leaders and employees in both voluntary and accountable ways in fostering inclusion and equity.

4. Regularly evaluate and adapt strategies to address new challenges and opportunities.

In summary, DEI BPs alone are insufficient to create lasting cultural transformation. A comprehensive, equity-centered organizational change strategy is essential for embedding equity-centered principles into an organization's fabric. Organizations can foster an inclusive culture that drives innovation, resilience, and long-term success by addressing systemic barriers, aligning efforts with organizational goals, and prioritizing sustainability. In an increasingly diverse and interconnected world, this approach is as much a moral imperative as a strategic business necessity.

Legal risk aversion is one threat to a robust ECDI framework designed to drive culture change. An example is when an organization avoids collecting quantitative survey data, especially when participant demographics are collected. This results in a tendency to over-rely on interviews, focus groups, and benchmarking, which are considered safer. Ideally, benchmarking involves comparing an organization's DEI practices, outcomes, and metrics against industry standards. In practice, benchmarking provides a picture of where the organization stands relative to competitors regarding DEI efforts and helps identify gaps and opportunities for improvement.

When a needs assessment is limited to interviews and benchmarking, baseline data for measuring improvements over time is limited. The effort is also considered less trustworthy as the qualitative data too often falls victim to subjective instead of objective conclusions. Assessment is a continuous improvement of culture change, as it helps organizations identify areas for improvement, measure progress over time, and evaluate the effectiveness of change initiatives. Organizations can make informed decisions about the necessary changes to achieve their goals and enhance their overall performance and effectiveness. A high-impact ECDI initiative is based on a data-driven strategic plan designed to transform an organization by programmatically integrating equity-centered principles into its values, mission, and operations to achieve goals and objectives. Below is a true-to-life example of the difficulty in collecting rich data.

A non-profit organization that provides various psychiatric and psychosocial services recently acquired smaller competitor organizations to expand. While the organization had historically acquired an average of four competitors each year, its recent acquisitions reached eleven additional programs within a single year. This surge increased the number of employees and dramatically shifted workforce diversity. In response to these challenges, the COO proactively promoted inclusion throughout the system. The first step was to establish an equity and inclusion competency committee to implement and oversee a DEI initiative aimed at integrating diverse cultural groups.

I was teaching a graduate-level organizational development course at the time. I permitted a student working at the organization to use an assessment toolkit I developed for his organization's new "diversity initiative" as a class project. Although the toolkit included a survey, focus group, and key informant interview data collection tools, the equity and inclusion competency committee chose to use only the survey tool. The survey results were compared against the corresponding stages of the inclusion organizational change framework (as the stages were labeled at the time), and overall results indicated that the organization was in the Egalitarian Stage of inclusion. This was the next highest stage of inclusion in the framework at that time, signifying that the organization was performing well.

Excited about their organization's high score, the mostly historically majority and included group committee, particularly the COO, wanted to share it with the organization. However, for some committee members, especially BIPOCs serving on the committee, the results contradicted their personal experiences and views of the organization. The committee decided to contract with my consulting and training company to interpret the results. We evaluated their data and were surprised to learn that they calculated and used the overall survey results without breaking them down into results by demographic group. They also neglected to distribute the key informant and focus group instruments, even though the instructions require doing so. I reported to the committee that while the overall survey results provide one measure of the organization's stage of inclusion, the data were insufficient to give a full picture.

To address this issue, we segmented the survey data by departments, demographic groups, and organizational levels to uncover any group differences in the stages of inclusion among demographic categories, such as race, ethnicity, gender, job role, work location, and more. Additionally, we carried out key informant and focus group interviews. The supplementary data enhanced our interpretation by highlighting group differences. After gathering interview data, analyzing the survey data, and applying our method for integrating various data sources, the refined results revealed that the organization was, in fact, in the lower Defensive Stage of inclusion, which is two stages below the higher Egalitarian Stage. This real-world example illustrates the advantage of utilizing multiple sources and data analysis techniques in capturing a comprehensive array of voices to identify organizational gaps. Once the stage is identified, the interventions for culture change can be more effective.

Chapter 6: Building an Equitable, Culturally Diverse, and Inclusive Organization

ECDI provides a comprehensive and transformative approach. This approach critically examines the organization's values, policies, processes, and practices through the lens of equity and organizational change, enabling systemic changes based on data gathered from thorough assessments. The journey toward an ECDI culture begins with establishing a foundation for organizational change, crafting the culture change plan, executing the plan, and maintaining efforts until the mission is accomplished. The success of an ECDI initiative relies on a structured, intentional approach. Employees at the bottom of the hierarchy serve as the litmus test for assessing an equitable culture. The assumption is that if this segment of the workforce does not feel equity in the organization, it is likely that no one fully enjoys it, due to low equity and inclusion competency.

The initial steps in the initiative include appointing an expert practitioner to lead the effort, followed by creating a compelling, data-driven case to gain buy-in from leadership and middle management, and implementing a high-impact strategic culture change plan. The formation of a dedicated team and an equity and inclusion competency committee to support the initiative are equally essential, along with establishing mechanisms for sustaining the efforts that drive meaningful change. DEI BPs continue to play a role, but only to the extent that they integrate strategically within a data-driven, change-oriented strategy to achieve the most significant impact.

The ECDI Organizational Culture Change Approach

An ECDI organizational change approach emphasizes aligning the initiative with organizational goals and discovering ways to leverage cultural diversity to drive innovation, engagement, and equity. ECDI initiatives are rooted in data-driven strategies, clear objectives, and measurable outcomes. The organizational change goal is to foster a culture of equity by identifying and dismantling systemic barriers to equity. A combination of quantitative and qualitative data is collected, informed by input across the different segments and demographics within the organization. This dataset is then analyzed to identify strength areas, pinpoint barriers to equity, and establish baseline data for tracking cultural transformation over time. By systematically addressing these barriers in a culture change initiative, organizations can cultivate and promote success through a culture of equity and inclusion.

An assumption is that change does not happen quickly, and it is best understood as occurring in stages over time. The process of cultural transformation unfolds in key phases of initiative implementation: preparation, organizational assessment, strategic planning, implementation, and sustaining momentum. Each stage demands a focused strategy tailored to address its specific needs to ensure measurable progress. This section delves into the practices and critical thinking essential behind the ECDI approach to embarking on this transformational path. That starts with a team of experts.

Put an Equity, Cultural Diversity, & Inclusion Practitioner at the Helm

A key factor in preparing an ECDI initiative is having a competent practitioner in charge. Most presidents or CEOs undertaking a DEI initiative lack the necessary understanding of the complexities involved in the practitioner's role and the specific expertise it demands. They have little knowledge of the details of the DEI leader's job role or what constitutes competence in DEI work. This leads them to assign the responsibility to an employee who has shown success in other roles, understands the organization's culture, or has a reputation as an internal DEI champion for risk management purposes. While hiring someone who fits into the culture makes sense from a risk management standpoint, choosing an internal candidate without proper training or expertise can create more problems than solutions. This is why leaders are often inconsiderate of the practitioner's need for adequate training, staffing, and resources. The assumption that one person can handle all the tasks without support is unrealistic and sets them up for failure. Leaders would not set out to transform their organization's culture without expertise and a team of area specialists. They do not understand the enormity of the task or show appreciation for equity, cultural diversity, and inclusion expertise.

Too many internal DEI hires assume that being recruited by the leader and personal commitment to do good work are sufficient preparation. That is why only a handful seek credentialing training and those who do choose to "earn" a certification by passing a test in lieu of training from experts. After completing our certification program training, seasoned Fortune 500 company diversity officers have told us that they found value in the training and wished they had completed it earlier in their careers. Appointing a trained equity and inclusion competency practitioner provides the expertise needed for a successful initiative. Passing a test does not teach you how to onboard the leadership, devise a change strategy, measure success, etc. That requires learning from expert instruction and training.

Equity framework practitioners drive organizational change to foster a more equitable culture within institutions. With the proper support and resources, they can achieve organizational transformation. They bring the credibility, expertise, and interpersonal skills needed to build key relationships, cultivate trust, and ensure a positive and productive working environment. They guide an organization towards a cultural shift by effectively tackling issues, structural barriers, or leadership deficiencies that may hinder progress.

Change work cannot be successful with a one-person office taking the lead, even when they are fortunate enough to have the authority needed. They need staff, consultants, and other resources to manage and support the change initiatives. They may hire an organizational change expert, project manager, trainer, instructional designer, and personal assistant to support the initiative, but the equity and inclusion competency lead remains at the helm. That requires understanding the various areas of the work. The equity and inclusion competency change agent's expertise includes inclusion and equity competency, deploying a data-driven approach to analyzing the current system, identifying barriers to equity and inclusion, and closing competency gaps to facilitate change. They cannot get far without the influence skills needed to onboard senior leaders and middle- and lower-level managers. Otherwise, they will likely inadvertently undermine the ECDI initiative's effectiveness.

My mentor, Judith Katz, ED.D., emphasized the importance of partnering with an external expert in a conversation years ago. An external expert as a consultant can view the organization and its needs from a different vantage point, and they can present things like dysfunctional practices that may be too risky for the internal person to address. The internal person can more effectively navigate the organizational terrain and create connections that are difficult for the consultant. It is imperative that the internal person has strong leadership commitment and support, and partnerships with HR and EEO offices are nurtured.

The ECDI framework also emphasizes the integration of talent management within the change initiative, recognizing the need to maintain productivity amidst cultural transformation and the necessity of recruiting diverse talent to augment the change process. They understand how cultural differences can affect teamwork and the impact of historical marginalization and institutional barriers on the trust and productivity of marginalized groups, such as women and BIPOC employees. They establish a cycle of positive organizational change by crafting effective solutions and evaluating their effectiveness. Even though they may rely on contractors for specialized expertise, such as assessment, they understand enough about the different work areas to evaluate the contractors' contributions. By collaborating with their team, management, industry experts, vendors, and other partners, equity and inclusion competency practitioners use them as resources to foster a culture change.

They recognize the importance of integrating cultural diversity, equity, and inclusion into existing and emerging business models and everyday operations. They do so by applying an empathetic equity lens in their work. Their empathetic approach emphasizes ensuring that no segment of the workforce is left behind, regardless of their position within the organizational hierarchy or openness to the initiative. In this way, the ECDI initiative is essential to the organization's culture change success.

The changes initiated can foster cultural understanding and bridge differences, which enhances productivity, particularly during the change initiative. This underscores the critical role of equity and inclusion competency change agents in providing the expertise and knowledge needed to assist with internal issues, external forces, and operational processes while continuously promoting cultural diversity, equity, and inclusion. This makes them an essential resource that supports the organization and ensures the initiative's success. Next, a more detailed description of equity and inclusion competency practitioner characteristics is discussed.

CDEI Work is Challenging

All DEI roles are challenging. The equity and inclusion competency role is uniquely challenging due to the combination of the following factors:

1. Navigating Resistance and Opposition. Their initiatives often face resistance from within the organization, including skepticism from leadership, employees, or external stakeholders. Resistance stems from political polarization, cultural biases, or misunderstandings about the value of DEI. Equity and inclusion competency practitioners balance empathizing with those with oppositional views to avoid ostracizing them. They also hold people accountable to maintain momentum toward culture change.

Their initiatives also face threats from external sources, such as anti-DEI activist groups that pressure organizations to discontinue such efforts by sending demand letters. The equity and inclusion competency practitioner must support the organization through the turbulence without making concessions to the initiative.

2. Complexity of Cultural Transformation. Practitioners must be capable of transforming organizational culture to prioritize equity and inclusion with a long-term plan that includes a systemic change process. That means managing deeply ingrained biases, stereotypes, and invisible inequities such as unconscious bias. Unlike other leadership roles, equity and inclusion competency practitioners must directly confront sensitive issues, such as racism, equity and fairness, gender disparities, and systemic inequities, which demand both emotional intelligence and resilience.

It is important to learn about and appreciate the natural resistance to change in order to affectively prepare for and address it. This involved deeply listening to all voices, but certainly those reflecting resistance to make certain that they feel heard.

3. Alignment with Strategic Goals. Practitioners must ensure that the ECDI initiatives are not siloed but integrated into the organization's overall strategic objectives. This requires cross-functional collaboration, stakeholder buy-in, and demonstrating how DEI contributes to business success.

4. Accountability and Metrics. Measuring the impact of DEI efforts is inherently complex, requiring both quantitative and qualitative measures to measure organizational change and its impact over time.

Equity and inclusion competency practitioners understand metrics, collect data, and how to present supporting data to justify the resources needed to sustain momentum.

5. Political and Legal Risks. ECDI work frequently intersects with changing legal standards and political dynamics, including internal affirmative action debates, anti-DEI legislation, and shareholder sentiment. They proactively safeguard against risks and manage them while maintaining the organization's reputation and compliance.

6. High-Stress Job Role. Equity and inclusion competency practitioners manage resistance and conflicts while addressing sensitive issues like discrimination, harassment, and deep-rooted inequities. They use self-care techniques and tools to manage the emotional labor the work demands.

7. Authority and Resources. They can only identify and present a clear picture of what can be realistically achieved within the confines of their budget, staffing, and support from the organization at large.

8. Diverse Skill Set Requirements. They must possess a rare combination of competencies, including strategic thinking, leadership, data-driven decision-making, financial acumen, and communication skills. Few other roles demand such a broad and nuanced skill set, but it can be learned with expert instruction and guidance

The equity and inclusion competency role stands out for its inherent challenges in driving systemic change, addressing deeply entrenched inequities, and fostering alignment across diverse stakeholders. These complexities make the position more demanding than many other leadership roles, requiring exceptional expertise, resilience, and adaptability.

In summary, an ECDI approach initially requires laying the groundwork for sustainable cultural transformation. Putting an equity and inclusion competency expert at the helm makes it possible to build the momentum needed for long-term success quickly. Through careful planning, organizations can cultivate a culture of equity, inclusion, and innovation. They should not be expected to do the work alone.

Characteristics of Equity, Cultural Diversity, and Inclusion Competency Expertise

Expert leadership is essential to transform an organization's culture through effective ECDI initiatives. The practitioner must possess strategic thinking, data-driven decision-making, communication, and change management expertise. What competencies are expected of equity and inclusion competency practitioners in their job roles? The roles of equity and inclusion competency practitioners and DEI practitioners are similar in that both involve leading efforts to foster inclusion and equity. However, the equity and inclusion competency practitioner's roles are distinct in that the former puts emphasis on creating a culture of equity, which assumes organizational change. This shifts the focus to efforts to achieve a desired state or culture.

The role also requires specific core competencies, such as leadership, financial acumen, and adaptability, to navigate complex organizational dynamics. Qualified practitioners know how to align cultural diversity, equity, and inclusion goals with broader organizational objectives, ensure initiatives are data-driven, and foster collaboration across teams. Political savvy is vital for managing resistance and external scrutiny, especially in polarized environments. A good example is the need to respond to the current attacks on DEI effectively. No one individual should be expected to do all the things needed to drive change. That makes it imperative to hire a team, utilize consultants in key areas, and identify and foster in-house partners.

A successful equity and inclusion competency practitioner skillfully transforms inequitable structures by embedding equity into organizational culture (e.g., inclusive and equitable communication skills and developing recruitment tools), dismantling equity barriers, and fostering an environment where roles and inclusion are no longer segmented by race, ethnicity, socioeconomic class, and gender. This role requires expertise in organizational assessment and aligning DEI initiatives with strategic goals.

The key responsibilities include, but are not limited to:

1. Developing and executing DEI strategies, policies, and training programs.

2. Leading organizational change to promote equity and inclusion.

3. Collaborating with executives to ensure DEI goals align with business objectives.

4. Managing diverse teams, increasing inclusion and equity competency across the organization, addressing resistance, and fostering inclusive cultures.

5. Developing, implementing, and monitoring DEI metrics to assess program effectiveness.

6. Ensuring their solutions and values comply with DEI-related legal standards and best practices.

The core competencies needed include:

1. Strategic Thinking: Aligning DEI initiatives with long-term organizational goals.

2. Leadership & Team Management: Inspiring teams, reducing conflict due to cultural differences, and managing resistance to change.

3. Communication: Developing and articulating data-driven goals, building trust, and fostering collaboration.

4. Decision-Making: Using data-driven insights to address complex challenges, such as effectively onboarding the organization to complete inclusion and equity competency training.

5. Change Management: Leading cultural transformations with adaptability and resilience.

6. Metrics and Measurement: Using valid and reliable tools and basic statistics.

7. Political Savvy: Navigating resistance and external scrutiny effectively.

8. Inclusion and equity competency: Promoting cultural diversity and equity across the organization.

By mastering these responsibilities and competencies, equity and inclusion competency practitioners are pivotal in driving systemic change, enhancing organizational performance, and fostering a culture of equity and inclusion. By hiring and investing in trained, certified, and competent leaders, organizations can achieve sustainable cultural change and effectively navigate today's dynamic and challenging DEI landscape.

The list of things they are expected to and need to be able to do is daunting. Training can increase competencies across the areas over time. However, the list also indicates that the practitioner should not be able to do all of these things alone. They need a staff that complements their expertise to be most effective, avoid burnout, and allow space to work on higher-level tasks and organizational needs.

In summary, equity and inclusion competency supports driving meaningful change and aligning organizational goals with equity and diversity initiatives. This skill set ensures that they can meet the demands of today's complex and dynamic organizational landscapes. Equity and inclusion competency practitioners require a set of competencies to drive organizational change and foster inclusive environments. Key skills include strategic thinking to align ECDI goals with long-term objectives, leadership to inspire teams and manage resistance, and decision-making based on data-driven insights. Effective communication and operational excellence are essential for articulating goals and optimizing workflows, while financial acumen ensures sustainable ECDI initiatives. These core competencies equip a DEI leader to navigate the complexities of organizational change, foster a culture of belonging, and achieve measurable progress in diversity, equity, and inclusion efforts.

Staff the Equity, Cultural Diversity, and Inclusion Competency Office with a Team of Specialists

An equity and inclusion competency practitioner seeks to hire specialists whose expertise complements their own to create a well-rounded DEI office. The staff ensures the office has the capacity to address the full range of the initiative's needs. The key areas and specializations include (1) training design and development, (2) data analysis and metrics, (3) employee engagement and well-being, (4) recruitment and talent management (including accessibility and disability), (5) communications and brand specialist, (6) change management, (7) equity strategy and innovation, and (8) and community engagement. A staff member proficient in more than one specialist area is certainly ideal. An organization may have unique needs that require other specializations not listed, such as experience working in an employee union environment. By assembling a diverse team with complementary expertise, the leader ensures that all aspects of diversity, equity, and inclusion are addressed holistically to drive meaningful and sustainable organizational change.

Create an Organizational Change Committee

The change committee is crucial for designing, developing, and implementing an organization's high-impact ECDI initiative. The practitioner brings the committee members together to create a strategic and continuous improvement plan and implement initiatives that foster greater fairness in the workplace. The committee's main role is to provide leadership and guidance for developing and implementing the plan. The members are responsible for working directly with the equity and inclusion competency lead in setting goals and objectives, creating a strategic plan, and monitoring their progress. It must be culturally diverse, and their work with the committee needs to be part of their job responsibilities, rather than an extra assignment they are expected to do over and beyond that role. The leadership selects them, rather than asking for volunteers.

The committee also provides a platform for sharing ideas, best practices, and resources. One of the benefits of the equity and inclusion competency committee is that it brings together individuals from various backgrounds and perspectives. A diverse committee ensures that different viewpoints and experiences are considered when designing the initiative, resulting in a more comprehensive and inclusive approach. The committee members also act as advocates and ambassadors for equity, cultural diversity, and inclusion competency within the organization. They help raise awareness about the initiative's importance, educate employees about terms and concepts, and address related issues or concerns. By actively promoting the committee can support onboarding the larger organization to the initiative and help create a more equitable, inclusive, and respectful work environment where individuals feel valued and respected for their different and unique backgrounds and contributions.

When recruiting committee members, the leader identifies and selects individuals within the organization who are passionate about workplace equity and committed to driving change. They aim to recruit representation from different departments, job roles, levels, and backgrounds to ensure diverse perspectives and experiences. They develop and broadcast a call for volunteers, inviting specific individuals to join the committee with clear information about its purpose and the people being recruited. A recruitment tool that articulates the desired proficiencies is created and utilized to provide objectivity and transparency.

A common mistake many equity and inclusion competency practitioners and committees make is avoiding individuals who openly oppose the initiative. While many dissenters should indeed be avoided due to their reputation for not collaborating effectively in teams, some dissenting voices genuinely seek to understand how the work aligns with organizational goals. Opposition to equity, cultural diversity, and inclusion competency within the organization among the workforce often stems from a lack of understanding and prevailing myths. When an employee's objections to the initiative seem sincere, they can be ideal committee members. Including at least one individual who openly questions the committee's credibility and value is crucial. There's nothing to fear.

As mentioned, the individual's objections likely arise from a genuine concern for the organization's well-being and success, especially management. Other members of the organization may share similar objections and misunderstandings, so having a "dissenter" on the committee amplifies those voices. These "resisters" can assist the committee in determining how to address resistance to change within the workforce. Once on the committee, the member's perspective can aid in preparing for potential pushback from the larger organization. They serve as the committee's eyes, ears, and allies. By actively promoting the initiative, the committee can onboard more members of the organization.

Another clear benefit of having the equity and inclusion competency committee is that it helps ensure the project's sustainability and long-term success. The committee members can assist in assessing the initiative's effectiveness, gather employee feedback, and offer suggestions for making necessary adjustments to increase its impact and effectiveness. They can also identify areas for growth and development, such as implementing diversity training programs or expanding recruitment efforts to attract a more diverse talent pool.

The equity and inclusion competency practitioner should define the committee's purpose, leaving the committee to define its role and ground rules for working together. The practitioner facilitates and starts the committee's work with a clearly defined purpose and objectives. This provides clear direction for the committee's work and ensures everyone is on the same page.

Chapter 7: Building a Culture of Equity Through Strategic Organizational Change

In an increasingly diverse and interconnected world, creating a culture of equity within organizations is more than a moral imperative. It is a strategic necessity for modern organizations. Equity ensures that all individuals, regardless of their background, have fair access to opportunities, resources, and support needed to thrive. Yet, fostering a culture of equity requires more than good intentions, especially in hierarchical, culturally diverse organizations with institutionalized inequities. Transformation needed to increase equity demands deliberate and systematic change.

Transforming an organization's culture to prioritize equity involves addressing deeply ingrained practices and policies with a strategic vision for inclusion and fairness. By integrating an organizational culture change plan with an ECDI strategic and continuous improvement plan, leaders can establish a clear roadmap for embedding equity into the very fabric of their organization. This combined approach ensures that equity initiatives are not siloed but interwoven with broader organizational goals, creating sustainable impact.

This section discusses how organizations can embark on a transformative journey to cultivate an equity-centered culture. From evaluating current practices to implementing actionable strategies and integrating equity into long-term goals, this approach serves as a guide for leaders dedicated to impactful change. It explores the relationship between organizational culture and culture change strategy, providing practical insights for fostering an equitable and inclusive environment where every individual can bring their whole selves to an organization in the service of productivity. An organizational change method is needed to guide the effort.

The ECDI Framework of Organizational Change

Changing an organization's culture requires a structured approach that supports sustainable change. Understanding the current stage of equity, cultural diversity, and inclusion is critical for determining where an organization is on the culture change continuum. Lower stages represent organizations with more performance gaps than those in higher stages. Each stage offers insights into the organization's strengths and challenges on its path to greater equity.

Several popular change models exist, but two have influenced the ECDI framework. Perhaps the most popular is Kotter's Organizational Change Framework, developed by the organizational change expert Dr. John Kotter. This eight-step model is designed to guide organizations through successful change initiatives. It emphasizes creating urgency, empowering broad-based action to remove obstacles to change, and making short-term victories. The ten-step Kotter organizational change process is summarized below.

1. Assess the Current Culture to Identify the Current Stage, Gaps, and Barriers. The objective is to understand the existing organizational culture, its strengths, and areas for improvement. Analyze the data to identify cultural norms, values, and behaviors currently defining the organization.

2. Identify Gaps and Barriers. This step identifies discrepancies between the current and desired culture to identify the gaps between the new culture and those aspects of the current culture that create change obstacles (e.g., outdated policies and procedures, management resistance, and toxic behaviors).

3. Develop a Culture Change Plan. This step lays out a roadmap for achieving the desired culture. Specifying measurable goals for cultural change, providing the right tools, and encouraging participation are common in this phase.

4. Define the Desired Culture. Next, establish a clear vision for the new culture that aligns with organizational goals and values. This involves

collaborating with leadership to articulate core values and behaviors for the desired culture. To foster buy-in, employees are involved in defining the desired culture.

5. Engage Leadership and Key Stakeholders. This step involves reinforcing leadership commitment and establishing a culture change equity and inclusion competency committee with representatives from different departments and across the organizational chart. Ensuring the leadership and executives model the desired cultural behaviors. This often requires training leaders to role model the new culture's behaviors.

6. Communicate the Vision. Engage the entire organization by fostering awareness and understanding of the cultural change initiative while helping them recognize the benefits of supporting the change. Establish a communication strategy that includes regular updates, town halls, and Q&A sessions.

7. Implement Key Initiatives. Completing this step is essential for implementing tangible actions that can foster the desired culture. This involves addressing gaps and barriers, such as revising and creating policies, processes, and systems (e.g., performance reviews and hiring practices) that align with the desired culture.

8. Monitor Progress. This step evaluates the effectiveness of cultural change efforts. Metrics (e.g., employee satisfaction, retention rates, and productivity) are established to track progress.

9. Reinforce and Sustain the Culture. Making the products of the initiative a lasting part of the organization is operationalized by integrating them into the initiative's goals, mission, and operations. Embed inclusion competence culture values into onboarding, performance management, and daily operations. Continuously recognize and celebrate cultural milestones to reinforce the efforts.

10. Address Challenges Proactively. Overcoming resistance and maintaining momentum is an ongoing effort until the new culture becomes how things are expected to be done.

The above steps of Kotter's change framework offer a structured, ten-step method for driving organizational transformation.

By focusing on assessing the current culture to identify gaps and creating a clear vision for change, the Kotter framework aims to create a shift toward lasting change. Key steps include engaging leadership, communicating the vision to foster organizational buy-in, implementing targeted initiatives to align policies and practices with desired outcomes, and monitoring progress through measurable metrics. The framework also emphasizes the importance of celebrating short-term victories, reinforcing new cultural norms, and proactively addressing challenges to maintain momentum. Using Kotter's stage model increases the likelihood that change is embedded sustainably and becomes an integral part of the organization's culture.

The second stage model that influenced the ECDI framework is the Stages of Multicultural Organizational Development Framework (Jackson, B. W. (2006: Katz, J. H., & Miller, F. A., 1995). Their framework outlines the organization's journey as it shifts towards greater inclusion. This framework relies on identifying an organization's current diversity and inclusion integration status or stage to provide a structured approach for progressing toward a more inclusive culture. The journey towards an inclusive culture unfolds in six distinct stages within their framework. These stages range from the Exclusionary stage, where conformity to the dominant culture is expected, to the Redefining Organization stage, where social identity no longer dictates one's place in the organizational hierarchy—each person is, first and foremost, treated as a valued member of the organization.

The stages of the Multicultural Organizational Development Framework are:

- The Exclusionary Organization stage represents the lowest and most exclusive or monocultural stage. In this stage, diversity is resisted, and institutional policies, procedures, and practices exclude certain groups. An example is a practicing Catholic who owns an organization and sets it up to reflect their values, attempts to hire other Catholics and expects everyone to understand and adhere to Catholic values.

- The Club Organization reflects a "token" approach to diversity, allowing some diversity but prioritizing homogeneity and cultural fit over inclusion. A non-Catholic is hired and expected to fit into the culture as is and, ideally, will feel compelled to convert.

- The Compliance Organization focuses on legal compliance and policies that prevent discrimination. Diversity is recognized but not fully integrated into the culture. An example is ensuring that non-Catholic employees are not subjected to unfair treatment in compliance with the law.

- The Affirming Organization actively supports diversity and may have implemented DEI, but it typically views the programs and projects as separate from core operations. Employee resource groups, for example, are implemented to provide employees of other faiths with a safe space to interact with each other.

- The Redefining Organization - Recognizes the value of diversity and starts embedding it into policies, practices, and business goals, viewing it as essential for success. The organization's Catholic culture undergoes rethinking and change to incorporate a more inclusive work environment.

- The Inclusive Equity Organization fully integrates diversity and inclusion into all its aspects. This stage represents a truly inclusive culture where diverse perspectives are actively valued, and everyone feels they belong.

Varying attitudes, behaviors, and organizational practices define each distinct stage. In the initial stage, the Exclusionary Organization, the organization is predominantly people who look the same and share a similar culture (monocultural). The organization indirectly and often directly expresses pride in maintaining the status quo. Diversity is actively resisted. Any existing diversity, for example, a Latino or a woman, is relegated to low-level jobs and paid less. Policies and practices actively exclude certain groups, for example, non-Christians.

Reaching the Inclusive Equity organization stage represents the pinnacle of this progression, where diversity is deeply ingrained in every aspect of the organization's operations, fostering innovation, performance, and engagement, and there is an ongoing commitment to equity and inclusion. The leadership constantly questions the status quo. Do we have the right people in this discussion? Who else needs to be included in order to make the right decision? What perspectives, experiences are missing? Do our policies and practices enable each person to contribute their best work? Honest and data-driven answers to those questions drive change.

The Multicultural Organizational Development Framework loosely influenced the development of the ECDI framework. The ECDI framework is based on a five-stage organizational development model, thus differing in the number of stages and what needs to happen to shift an organization's culture. The chart summarizes the stages.

Figure 1: Stages of Becoming an Equitable, Culturally Diverse, and Inclusion Competency Organization

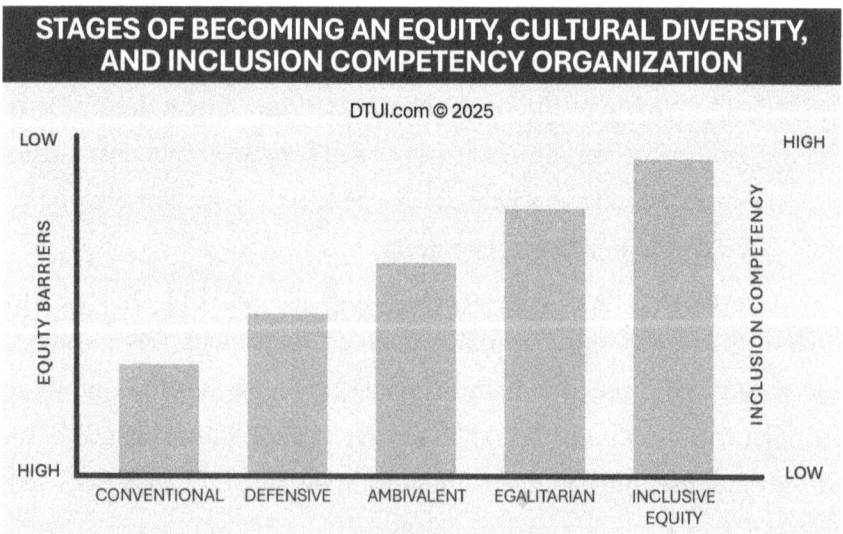

STAGES OF BECOMING AN EQUITY, CULTURAL DIVERSITY, AND INCLUSION COMPETENCY ORGANIZATION

DTUI.com © 2025

The ECDI framework assumes that stages are traversed as a result of organizational improvements in equity and inclusion practices and competence. The stages include:

1. Conventional Stage: Everyone in the organization is expected to conform to the dominant culture in this stage, as the management is most comfortable with a workforce made up of people similar in their values and views, including cultural and racial backgrounds. Most of the members tend to share racial identity and values. To the extent that there are historically marginalized and excluded groups in the workforce, they are relegated to lower-level jobs. They regularly experience microinequities and microaggressions with little recourse within the organization due to structural barriers and low equity and inclusion competency. The leadership and management tend to be high in Social Dissonance Orientation or SDO.

2. Defensive Stage: The need for legal compliance is the leading reason for shifting the organization to this stage, rather than internal changes in values. Opportunities to secure government contracts that require contractors to implement, regulate, and report equal employment opportunity and affirmative action policies and procedures are examples. An equal employment lawsuit is often another reason. Awareness of the need for legal protection is heightened in this stage, creating the perception that DEI is a problem instead of a solution. The organization and leader are Moderate-High in Social Dissonance Orientation or SDO.

3. Ambivalent Stage: The organization is open to incorporating changes for greater inclusion, such as training, but resists structural change. This is the stage in which DEI BPs are fully embraced, especially to show tangible proof that the organization is changing. The human resource manager is more likely to support the leadership's efforts to maintain and reinforce existing structural inequities to maintain the culture. This organization suffers from ambivalent inclusion due to an underdeveloped equity and inclusion competency. There is recognition that fairness is essential and an organizational goal worthwhile pursuing.

DEI BPs are typically introduced in this stage. There may or may not be a DEI practitioner leading an initiative. DEI is cautiously implemented due to continued sensitivity to legal risk. The organization and leader are Moderate in Social Dissonance Orientation.

4. Egalitarian Stage: This organization may have received a diversity best practice award or feel confident about the results of its efforts to create an inclusive organization. While satisfied with the DEI BPs implemented, many hidden barriers to equity continue to exist, and there is lip service to openness to cultural changes needed to create equity. The organization is more willing to take risks when the positive impact of inclusion and increased competency pay off. The organization and leadership are Moderately Low in Social Dissonance Orientation.

5. Inclusive Equity Stage: The organization shifts from simply acknowledging diversity and inclusion to emphasizing the need for greater inclusion and equity competency, equitable systems and structures that promote fairness and equal opportunity, and uncovering the hidden equity barriers in processes, policies, and practices. An individual's racial and ethnic identities no longer determine where anyone falls on the organizational chart. The organization and leader are Low in Social Dissonance Orientation, and continuous improvement to sustain and improve the efforts.

The ECDI framework further assumes that (1) change occurs gradually in stages, (2) removing structural barriers to equity and increasing inclusion and equity competency are key to affecting change, (3) increasing equity and inclusion competency is critical for removing barriers to equity, and (4) high equity and inclusion and equity competency characterize culture change.

The Equity, Cultural Diversity, and Inclusion Competency framework uniquely emphasizes the removal of barriers to equity and increasing equity and inclusion competency as catalysts for change. The ECDI framework assumes that an organization's progression towards higher stages is a result of managing talent by increasing equity and inclusion competency and practices—that is, as inclusion and equity competency and institutional equity systems improve, the workforce experiences optimum performance and workforce sense of empowerment. The final assumption is that high levels of equity and inclusion competency reflect an equitable culture, as measured by those in the bottom strata enjoying inclusion and feeling more in relationship with those at the top and in the middle. Removing inequity barriers, providing targeted training, and normalizing allyship effectively boost inclusion and equity competency. This is imperative for creating an equitable and culturally diverse organization with high equity and inclusion competency.

Table 1: A description of the stages of creating an inclusive equity competency organization.

STAGES	DESCRIPTION
Conventional	Conforming; high social dominance orientation; very high in equity barriers
Defensive	Legal compliance; moderately high in social dominance orientation; moderately high in equity barriers
Ambivalent	Valuing cultural diversity; moderate in social dominance orientation; moderate in equity barriers
Egalitarian	Affirmative cultural diversity, moderately low in social dominance orientation; moderately low equity barriers
Inclusive Equity	High inclusion competence; low in social dominance orientation; low equity barriers.
Stage of Equity, Cultural Diversity, & Inclusion Competency Culture DTUI.com © 2025	

To summarize, culture change requires intentional strategies, including assessing current equity gaps, embedding inclusion into business practices, and equipping leadership with the competencies needed for sustainable change. ECDI offers a five-stage progression from a conventional, exclusionary workplace to one where equity and inclusion are fully integrated. The ECDI framework provides a structured approach to transforming organizational culture by equity and inclusion competency and removing systemic barriers. It emphasizes aligning talent management, employee needs, and business values to create a workplace where all employees experience a shared purpose and equitable opportunities. The implementation of the ECDI framework is discussed next.

Chapter 8: An Equity, Cultural Diversity, and Inclusion Competency Culture Change Approach

Changing an organization's culture is a strategic and structured process that requires commitment, clear goals, and collaboration at all levels. The ECDI framework is designed to increase organizational inclusion. Structural inclusion and Inclusion-Equity competency work together in bringing about change, based on the assumption that (1) culture change requires removing barriers that hinder the workforce from experiencing a shared purpose and a sense of equity and (2) there is creative coexistence among talent management, employee needs, and business values and goals.

Creating a harmonious balance among employees' personal values, workplace needs, and business values is essential for fostering engagement, loyalty, and organizational success. Aligning employee needs with business goals and objectives supports a relationship that thrives on mutual benefit and shared purpose. In that way, implementing ECDI considers employee aspirations to create synergy with the institution's mission. The goal is to establish a unified sense of purpose among the workforce and the leadership. Promoting work-life balance exemplifies how a company's talent management values can align with employees' personal needs and values, particularly in high-stress job roles. A creative coexistence perspective assumes that talent management, employee needs, and business goals are not mutually exclusive but rather complementary.

Fostering creative coexistence involves an ongoing dialogue between leadership, middle management, line workers, and stakeholders to refine practices, ensuring that business goals remain compatible with evolving employee needs and ECDI framework standards. One example is implementing a leadership development program that prioritizes learning about and showing appreciation for employee aspirations and considering ways to align them with organizational needs. Providing workforce training to develop inclusion and equity competency is another example.

In summary, hierarchical organizations tend to silo different segments, which results in a push and pull between the workforce and their workplace. Organizations thrive when they cultivate a culture that defeats the inequities in hierarchical organizations by embracing cultural differences, creating clear pathways for upward mobility, providing equitable opportunities, and aligning employee aspirations with organizational goals. This strategy produces a workplace driven by shared purpose, mutual respect, and sustainable growth. Central to a creative coexistence approach is the elimination of barriers that hinder the workforce's sense of shared purpose and their need to feel valued.

Culture Change Requires Removing Barriers to Equity

A hierarchical organization with a segmented, culturally diverse workforce is color-coded in terms of race and gender along the organizational chart, with the overrepresentation of historically marginalized and excluded groups at the bottom and historically majority and included groups at the top. The degree to which there is a creative coexistence relationship across the organizational segments determines how much those at the bottom feel included in the organization. The ECDI framework rests on the premise that removing structural barriers to equity increases productivity and engagement. This requires, in part, an equity audit to identify barriers and assess the degree they impact productivity at different levels of the organization. Note that there is no concerted effort to focus on any particular level of the organization. The assumption is that wherever inequity exists, everyone is negatively impacted in some way.

The ECDI characterizes equity and inclusion competency improvements along a continuum. The more structural barriers and poor equity and Inclusion competency, the lower an organization is in the maturity, or Equity, Cultural Diversity, and Inclusion Competency stage. The highest stage reflects a combination of high equity and Inclusion-Equity competency. Both historically marginalized and excluded groups and the historically majority and included group members feel a heightened sense of inclusion. A person's position along the hierarchy is no longer predictable by race and gender. Given that equity and inclusion competency encompasses the collective consciousness, attitudes, knowledge, and skills that enable individuals to cultivate and navigate a culturally diverse organization, it enables organizations to attenuate the hierarchy skillfully. Together, removing equity barriers and increasing equity and inclusion competency drive change. A strategy that puts the ECDI into action is necessary to change the culture.

The ECDI Four-Phase Organizational Culture Change Framework

Changing an organization's culture requires an action plan. The ECDI offers an organizational change plan that is systematically implemented. Implementing the ECDI framework involves four phases:

1. Preparing for the change initiative
2. Developing a culture change plan
3. Implementing the plans.
4. Sustaining the effort.

Each phase is grounded in proven methodologies for changing an organization's current culture to an envisioned culture of equity and inclusion. The framework emphasizes engaging stakeholders, taking actionable steps, modeling inclusion and equity competency, and consistently monitoring the culture change to ensure the transformation is rooted and sustained.

By following the plan and going through the phases, organizations can navigate the complexities of cultural change with clarity and purpose, driving progress toward a more inclusive and equitable environment. Next, each phase is explored, starting with the preparation steps that lay the foundation for success.

Preparation Phase

Launching an ECDI initiative involves an endeavor that takes a deliberate and structured approach to lay the groundwork for success. Preparation is not just about planning logistics. It also includes efforts to build trust and align in purpose, which reduce resistance and ensure alignment across all levels of the organization. The preparation phase is where the vision for the initiative starts to take shape, misconceptions are dispelled, and risk factors are identified to build momentum. This phase equips organizations with the clarity and focus needed to embark on a successful journey by identifying potential resistance needed to secure buy-in and trust from decision-makers. It prepares the work needed for high-impact ECDI initiative planning. Without careful preparation, even the most well-intentioned efforts risk falling short of making an impact.

Preparing for the initiative creates the foundation for success. The traditional DEI initiative begins with a kickoff meeting between the practitioner and key stakeholders, including the top leader and management team members, to set the tone for the initiative and ensure alignment on goals, expectations, and responsibilities. This meeting is a crucial step in launching the ECDI initiative, as it establishes a shared understanding of its strategic importance and outlines the approach for collaboration and accountability. The kickoff meeting is successful when participants agree about the initiative's objectives, scope, and expected outcomes. The meeting offers the best opportunity to reinforce the importance of the leadership's role in driving and supporting the initiative, identify how each stakeholder will contribute to its success, develop accountability measures, and build trust and transparency. These are the common features of strategic and continuous planning preparation. Additional preparation is needed when centering equity in the work.

The ECDI approach starts with selecting an expert to lead the initiative, creating a business case for organizational change, and identifying an organizational change framework. It is not that typical planning does not include these. The point is that they are highlighted and occur strategically in the ECDI approach. The remainder of this section summarizes the prework in the strategic planning phase. By addressing key factors such as building a compelling business case, onboarding leadership, selecting an organizational change model, assembling a committee framework, and developing an ECDI Mission-Driven Inclusion Map, the preparation phase lays the groundwork for meaningful kickoff meeting discussion of the initiative's goals and needs.

A real-life example underscores the importance of additional preparation in planning for inclusion and equity culture change. A diversity officer in a healthcare organization sought to gather data to provide insights into the organization's DEI needs. They hired us to conduct the assessment. Key representatives from the diversity office, led by the diversity officer, attended the project kickoff meeting. The client shared that the CEO was enthusiastic about collecting data to identify gaps to address them. After the meeting, and before we could get our work started, the diversity officer informed us that there were problems with continued leadership support. After consultations with the human resources manager and legal team, the CEO was advised to not move forward with the assessment to manage legal risks. Their joint professional opinion was that collecting data about employee experiences and sorting the results into cultural and racial groups could expose the organization to legal risks should the results prove unfavorable.

The human resource manager and legal officer correctly concluded that any relevant existing data is subject to discovery in potential legal cases involving the organization's practices. Existing documents, data, or other information (including assessment data) deemed relevant to a legal suit can be subject to disclosure for a case against the organization. Their low-risk tolerance is understandable but shortsighted. Failing to implement solutions to safeguard against inequities in a hierarchical organization has proven to consistently result in historically marginalized and excluded group grievances that harm the organization's reputation and bottom line. Not collecting the data thus puts the organization at risk as well. Fortunately, the diversity officer reported directly to the CEO. Despite caution from legal and human resources officers, the leader allowed the diversity officer to collect data. This underscores the necessity of having the DEI practitioner report directly to the CEO.

DTUI collected and analyzed the survey assessment and interview data and interpreted the results to identify the organization's developmental stage. The diversity officer determined from the assessment report and recommendations which solutions were necessary to address identified performance gaps. Several years later, they aimed to reassess the organization to determine if it had reached higher inclusion stages. The CEO conferred with the legal and human resources officers again. They were more concerned at this point because comparisons between the original assessment outcomes and the subsequent assessment result may prove unfavorable to the organization, and that information would then be documented as evidence of the persistence of inequities. The CEO decided not to allow the second assessment to manage risk. This illustrates an organization's risk-averse nature and how it can impact DEI work. The ECDI approach requires early assessment of the leadership and upper management's resistance to devise strategies for successfully onboarding them.

Had the diversity officer used an ECDI approach, they would have met with the leader and upper management, including the human resource manager and the equal opportunity office, to discuss the need for collecting data before seeking the CEO's final approval to conduct the assessment. What is learned from those meetings about resistance and its sources provides insights into crafting a persuasive argument, minimizing pushback, and securing their buy-in. This example highlights the importance of a proactive onboarding approach that includes identifying and managing resistance to increase the likelihood of a successful initiative. Adequate preparation for change initiatives is paramount for success.

An essential part of preparation is to put an expert at the helm and develop a committee to steer the work, which is assumed to have been done. The practitioner works with the committee to prepare a business case for organizational change, conduct the kickoff meeting, collect data, develop a strategic and continuous improvement plan, and implement it. Each is discussed below.

Creating a Business Case for Culture Change

The practitioner must present a compelling business case for implementing the ECDI initiatives. Developing a robust business case articulating the rationale and benefits for undergoing change is crucial for preparing the organization for the journey. A well-crafted business case serves as a roadmap for change, outlining the strategic objectives, anticipated outcomes, and key performance indicators. It provides stakeholders with a clear understanding of the value proposition of culture change and its alignment with the organization's strategic priorities.

A Mission-Driven ECDI Map visually illustrates the connections among an organization's success goals, mission and vision, operational strategies, and inclusion and equity competency. This makes it imperative for onboarding leadership to the ECDI initiative. It helps to foster leadership buy-in and clarify how inclusion and equity competency aligns with the organization's purpose and priorities to drive success. Leaders enhance their understanding of how promoting initiative contributes to achieving operational and strategic objectives, such as employee retention, innovation, customer satisfaction, and market expansion. Here is how to build a map.

Creating a Mission Driven Strategy Map

Critical to success is determining what is needed to improve organizational effectiveness, such as in operations. Also recognizing where the organization is performing well such as in innovation, product development, customer service, etc. This directly ties the ECDI work to what really matters to the organization. An ECDI strategy map is useful for this purpose.

Once the practitioner is appointed, the committee collaborates with them to develop a Mission-Driven Inclusion Map. It requires linking the factors that are assumed to make the organization successful, such as the mission and vision, with inclusion and equity competencies needed to achieve that success. The result is a visual illustration of how inclusion and equity competency contribute to an organization's bottom line.

A strategy map visually links an organization's success drivers across four interconnected levels to show cause-and-effect relationships. The Mission-Driven Inclusion Map uses four layers or rows in a chart as labeled below:

- Bottom Line (Top row): The ultimate goal and business outcomes.
- Mission and Vision (Second Row): The guiding purpose and strategic goals.
- Operations (Third Row): The core internal processes and actions that drive results.
- The Last Inclusion, Equity, and Competence (Bottom Row): The foundational elements that impact operations, and the other levels as a result.

A blank column to the right of the row label is for the information generated when completing the map. By structuring the strategy map this way, the results represent how the inclusion competency approach plays a key role in organizational performance and the need for an ECDI initiative to improve the bottom line. An example of results is shown below. The company, APIC, used as an example is not real.

Figure 2: An example of a completed Mission-Driven Strategy Map

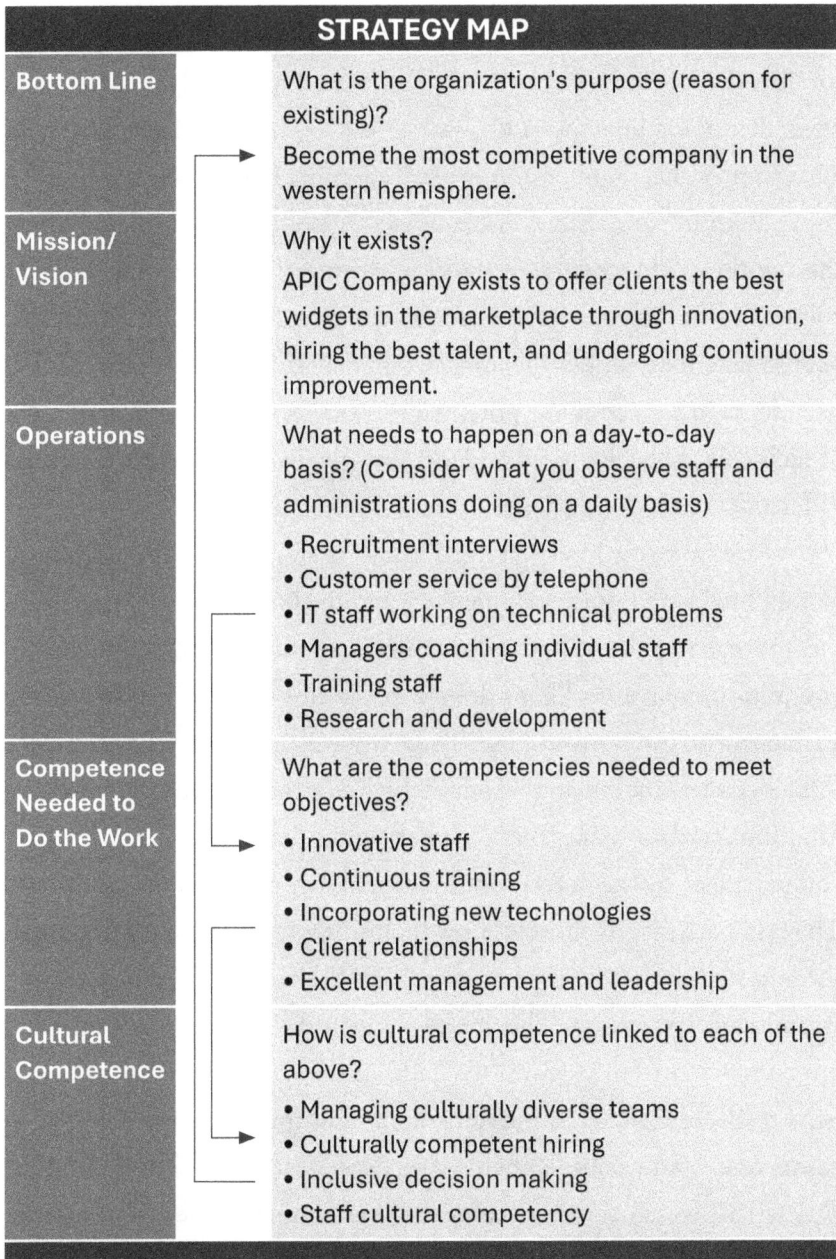

STRATEGY MAP	
Bottom Line	What is the organization's purpose (reason for existing)? Become the most competitive company in the western hemisphere.
Mission/ Vision	Why it exists? APIC Company exists to offer clients the best widgets in the marketplace through innovation, hiring the best talent, and undergoing continuous improvement.
Operations	What needs to happen on a day-to-day basis? (Consider what you observe staff and administrations doing on a daily basis) • Recruitment interviews • Customer service by telephone • IT staff working on technical problems • Managers coaching individual staff • Training staff • Research and development
Competence Needed to Do the Work	What are the competencies needed to meet objectives? • Innovative staff • Continuous training • Incorporating new technologies • Client relationships • Excellent management and leadership
Cultural Competence	How is cultural competence linked to each of the above? • Managing culturally diverse teams • Culturally competent hiring • Inclusive decision making • Staff cultural competency

The first step is to fill in the information for each row. The measurable results that define success are listed. These often include increased revenue, improved customer satisfaction, employee retention, and risk reduction. The leadership helps to decide the bottom line. The organization's formal mission and vision statements are restated in the second step. The third row lists the core business processes. This is what we visually point towards when describing to an outsider what employees do on a daily basis, such as recruiting, meetings, customer service, product development, etc. The last or bottom row, Inclusion Competency, content results from asking the question, "How might an ability to work with people across different cultures in the organization be associated with each operation listed?" For recruitment, for example, the information may indicate that recruiters will need to learn how to make potential recruits feel comfortable regardless of their cultural background and identify talent across a range of cultural differences.

Once each row has been filled, the next step is to establish linkages among Inclusion Equity Competency and the bottom line. First, draw a link for each item listed in the third row, Operations, to the row, Mission and Vision, above it. Then, draw a single line from the Mission and Vision row to the Bottom Line. These results show how the Operations influence the Mission and Vision, which in turn influence the Bottom Line. Finally, draw a line from each item in the list of equity and inclusion competencies to the corresponding operation in the Operations row. The result is a map that shows how Inclusion Equity Competency drives the bottom line. The competency impacts the operations, which impact the mission and vision. The areas in which the competency is needed but does not currently exist provide insights into performance gaps that need to be addressed. Improvements in cultural diversity recruitment competency, for example, increase the organization's ability to hire the best talent, which then increases the operational efficiency needed to carry out the mission in ways that positively impact the bottom line.

This strategy map clearly shows that the ECDI initiative is central rather than separate from the business strategy. When organizations invest in CDEI, operational efficiency, employee engagement, and customer loyalty improve, ultimately leading to stronger financial performance and a competitive advantage. The resulting map supports making a case for the need to take the initiative seriously and highlights its benefits. By following these steps, organizations can create a map that effectively communicates the importance and impact of an ECDI initiative.

In summary, a Mission-Driven Strategy Map visually the relationship between inclusion competency and organizational success, enabling leadership to recognize the strategic significance, practical advantages, and actionable steps necessary for cultivating an inclusive culture. This alignment not only secures buy-in but encourages leaders to engage in promoting and sustaining the ECDI initiative. Leaders and management find the map easy to understand and valuable for discussing risk from a positive perspective. It serves as a bridge to conversations about resource allocation needs and opportunities for enhancing Inclusion Competency. Additionally, the map offers a flexible blueprint for navigating change and challenges while staying aligned with competency objectives.

Engaging the Leadership and Stakeholders

Once prepared, the Mission-Driven ECDI Strategy Map. helps the practitioner onboard the leadership team by walking the executives and top management through the results that visually align organizational goals with ECDI objectives. The ECDI practitioner's goal is to foster understanding, commitment, and action. The process involves using the Mission-Driven Inclusion Strategy Map to connect the organization's mission, vision, and operational goals with inclusion and equity competency, illustrating the benefits and pathways for achieving an equitable and inclusive workplace. The map is of interest to the team as it demonstrates the direct linkages between inclusion and equity competency and broader organizational success goals, such as improved employee engagement, innovation, and customer satisfaction. This lays the groundwork for organizational change.

Ideally, the presenter facilitates the activity needed to create a Mission-Driven Inclusion Strategy Map. That is the most robust approach. In reality, it takes a bit of proficiency in designing and developing Mission-Driven Inclusion Strategy Maps to facilitate a group. That is why most choose to prepare the map beforehand and present the results in the chart. The meeting starts with reminding the participants about the initiative and introducing the discussion about the benefits for the organization and what's in it for them. Introduce the Mission-Driven Inclusion Strategy Map. and provide a general overview of its creation. Then, walk them through reading the map and the importance of the linkages across the rows depicted in arrows. Leadership can see how ECDI efforts integrate into the organization's mission and operational priorities.

Most find the map a good use of their time and insightful, especially given that Implementing DEI is discussed in terms of implementing solutions, such as equity and inclusion competency training for management and targeted recruitment practices. The discussions will likely involve clarifying how it is relevant to the organization. One way to help give them more insight is to ask them to come up with a few examples of operations and walk them through linking each with inclusion and equity competency. That gets their creative juices flowing and captures their hearts and minds. That involves breaking the technical aspects of the chart into meaningful, actionable, and measurable objectives, helping leadership team members understand how ECDI goals align with organizational success metrics.

The practitioner uses the map to demonstrate the importance of baseline data to identify existing competency gaps and areas requiring immediate attention, which helps them prioritize and allocate resources effectively. The meeting also provides an opportunity to introduce the importance of equity as complementary to inclusion and equity competency. The emphasis is on removing institutional barriers to equity, which requires inclusion competency and a commitment to fairness in the workplace to realize inclusion fully. In addition, discuss how an ECDI initiative is created and implemented in ways that protect the organization legally. End the presentation by focusing on tangible outcomes, such as increased innovation, better decision-making, higher retention, and enhanced reputation. Then, open the discussion to foster collaboration, ownership, and excitement.

Chapter 9: Create an ECDI Organizational Change Strategic Plan

Attacks on DEI in organizations and the shifting legal landscape require critical thinking about new ways of doing business. It fundamentally requires a change in talent management and inclusion practices. Changing an organization's culture requires a data-driven, strategic, structured approach with clear goals and strong, organization-wide commitment. A culture change plan is crucial when undergoing a major transformation, as the existing culture directly impacts strategy execution. Resistance often emerges during this process, revealing the organization's readiness to shift values, mindsets, and behaviors. The best chance for success is to identify the current organizational culture and develop an assessment report for use in strategic, continuous improvement planning.

A combination of strategic planning and continuous improvement planning is essential for creating an equitable and inclusive culture. Organizations need to address both the long-term vision and the ongoing realities of systemic change, especially those with considerable barriers to inclusion. Strategic planning provides a clear roadmap by defining the organization's long-term goals, priorities, and resource commitments for the initiative. It establishes a shared vision, accountability structures, and measurable outcomes that signal leadership's commitment to transforming the culture. Due to the nature of equity and inclusion work, entrenched barriers like bias, exclusionary practices, and power imbalances across cultures in the organization, barriers cannot be eliminated with a one-time plan. Continuous improvement is necessary to ensure progress stays adaptive, responsive, and sustainable.

The culture change plan represents a comprehensive, data-driven strategy for integrating equity and inclusion competency principles into an organization's mission, vision, values, policies, and operations. It serves as a roadmap for fostering an equitable workplace culture where all employees feel engaged and valued. The plan outlines clear goals, actionable strategies, and measurable outcomes needed to dismantle systemic barriers, enhance equity, and create an environment where employees can thrive and contribute. It includes initiatives that promote fair treatment, access, and opportunities, ensuring that equity remains a core aspect of the organization's culture, operations, and long-term sustainability. While equity for all employees is the central focus, addressing the unique needs of historically marginalized and excluded group members is essential, as their perception of equity is a key indicator of the plan's success. The plan highlights accountability, continuous improvement, and alignment with organizational needs and objectives.

The ECDI approach combines culture change and strategic, continuous improvement planning to ensure alignment between business goals and workplace culture. It is assumed that change is necessary and that resistance to DEI is normal. Integrating the culture change plan into the strategic plan is the best way to address resistance strategically. The strategic, continuous improvement change plan focuses on shifting organizational values, behaviors, and practices to align with business objectives and external changes with a long-term vision, goals, and priorities, focusing on overall mission, growth, operations, and resource allocation. The ECDI approach combines the two in a set of practical steps designed to bring about cultural change.

The eight-step approach to designing a strategic cultural transformation plan includes:

1. Selecting an organizational change model.
2. An assessment to identify the current organizational culture.
3. Identifying the current stage of ECDI culture.
4. Create an assessment report.
5. Create a strategic, continuous improvement report.
6. Develop a continuous improvement plan.

7. Create a communication plan.

8. Create an implementation plan.

Each step is summarized below.

Step 1: Select a Culture Change Framework

Organizational culture change requires a structured approach to transform the existing culture successfully. The ECDI change framework simplifies this complex process by breaking it down into manageable steps, ensuring a smoother transition. As previously discussed, this stage model framework characterizes an organization's progressive transformation toward greater equity and inclusion competency. The framework assumes that organizations advance through stages, with each stage representing an increase in inclusion competency, which reflects a cultural change resulting in stage overlap. Traces of the previous stage characteristics may be present in the subsequent stage as the organization matures. A summary of the stages is as follows:

1. In the lower Conventional Stage, the organization actively maintains and promotes a culture that favors historically majority and included group males, and all employees are expected to conform. The workforce is largely homogeneous, with historically marginalized and excluded groups relegated to lower-level positions and experiencing microinequities and microaggressions without a safety net. Equity barriers are prevalent, and Inclusion Competency is minimal.

2. The Defensive Stage follows. External pressures, such as George Floyd's death protests in the media and employee demands (internal pressures) for the organization to support the protesters' cause, result in public commitment with little more than surface change (e.g., creating and filling a DEI job role). Internal resistance to inclusion efforts is prevalent, with any existing DEI initiative implemented primarily for legal compliance or meeting compliance with government contracts

requirements rather than internal commitment. There is an increased awareness of inclusion due to demographics rather than planned. Existing organizational inequities are not assessed or viewed as essential for organizational success.

3. The Ambivalent Stage organization embraces DEI awareness and commitment but resists deep structural change. The top leader understands that DEI is a bottom-line driver and commits to making the organization more inclusive. The human resource managers and legal officers often resist DEI due to perceived legal risks, preferring to reinforce existing norms and resist change. Fairness is recognized as necessary and desirable and based on equality assumptions. This results in a cautious approach to implementing DEI initiatives. DEI BPs are considered the safer approach due to aligning with other organizations. A DEI practitioner position may or may not exist. The organization's DEI initiative is most vulnerable to lawsuits at this stage due to prioritizing equality instead of equity.

4. Organizations in the Egalitarian Stage have implemented DEI BPs to the extent that it is possible to compete in best practices award competitions. Some barriers to equity continue to exist. Successfully winning the award can lead to complacency, reinforcing the belief that no further action is needed. Inequities remain, but they are difficult to address, and the award is assumed sufficient for legal protection. That is why organizations in this stage are not immune to equity lawsuits, such as those related to salary and promotions. While programs are in place, the commitment to deep cultural change needed to remove equity barriers remains surface-level, creating a barrier to true equity.

5. In the Equity and Inclusion Competency stage, organizations continue to actively reduce biases and dismantle structural barriers to equity for ongoing improvement. Everyone in the organization receives annual training to continuously learn equity and inclusion competency. Policies and systems are intentionally crafted to promote fairness, ensuring that historically marginalized and excluded groups experience a fair and equitable workplace.

The ECDI approach, in summary, asserts that (1) organizational change happens gradually through these stages, (2) equity is achieved by removing structural barriers and improving Inclusion Competency, and (3) a truly equitable organizational culture is characterized by high structural equity and Inclusion Competency. Identifying the current stage requires collecting and analyzing data that uncovers structural barriers and competency gaps.

Step 2: Assessment to Identify the Current Culture

The assessment is a structured process that evaluates an organization's current stage of ECDI culture. Taylor Cox, Jr., a DEI pioneer, emphasized the importance of establishing baseline data and benchmarking to measure progress, identify gaps, and ensure accountability in reaching what was at the time referred to as cultural diversity goals. Our approach follows this same principle and uses the term cultural diversity. The ECDI assessment offers a comprehensive, data-driven approach to assessing an organization's culture. It incorporates multiple data collection methods to provide a well-rounded understanding of an organization's equity and inclusion competency. It is designed to identify barriers, competency gaps, and opportunities for cultural change using the following action plan:

- Collecting Data – Gather quantitative and qualitative information from employees and organizational systems to establish a baseline.
- Analyzing the Data Gathered – Identify patterns, gaps, and opportunities for improvement.
- Identifying Competency Gaps – Determine where the organization falls short in equity and Inclusion Competency, and its areas of strength.
- Creating the Assessment Report – Document the key insights, findings, and recommendations to guide decision-making and action planning.

- <u>Reassessing to Measure Progress</u> – Periodically tracking changes after implementing the strategic culture change plan to evaluate the effectiveness of initiatives and adjust strategies as needed.

By completing these actions, organizations can develop an effective ECDI framework that drives meaningful change and creates an equitable workplace culture.

Dr. Edward E. Hubbard has also contributed significantly to the development of structured assessment processes, particularly in the realm of diversity, equity, and inclusion within organizational settings. One of his notable contributions is the creation of the Seven-Level Diversity ROI Analysis Framework, which provides a systematic approach for DEI practitioners to measure and demonstrate the return on investment for initiatives. This framework emphasizes the importance of linking diversity efforts to tangible business outcomes, enabling organizations to assess the effectiveness of their DEI strategies through metrics such as benefit-to-cost ratios, payback periods, and return on expectations. (Hubbard, E. E., 2003).

Dr. Hubbard's work underscores the necessity of isolating the impact of diversity initiatives from other organizational factors to attribute outcomes accurately. By doing so, organizations can validate the specific contributions of DEI programs to overall performance, fostering greater accountability and strategic alignment. In summary, regular reassessments ensure continuous progress, accountability, and continuous improvement.

The ECDI assessment collects data from four key sources using specialized tools for an equity audit, key informant interviews, focus group interviews, and survey data collection. The result is a systematic review of policies, procedures, and practices, dialogues with individuals and groups of participants, and gathering workforce experiences through surveys. By using multiple distinct methods—document analysis, two types of interviews, and a survey—and triangulating the results, the study enhances the credibility of the findings through cross-validation, thereby increasing reliability. This multi-method approach provides a holistic view of an organization's ECDI landscape, helping to identify targeted, impactful strategies for long-term cultural transformation.

Equity Audit. An equity audit analyzes an organization's records to identify disparities in policies, practices, and outcomes. The goal is to uncover systemic inequities and areas for improvement. This process involves reviewing historical documents such as employee policies, training materials, recruitment and promotion data, marketing materials, and organizational reports. By examining these records, organizations can assess past and present talent management practices, identify patterns of inequities, and determine how well their efforts align with DEI objectives. Key sources for an equity audit include grievance and harassment policies, mission and values statements, hiring and promotion data across different identity groups, demographic information, supplier diversity programs, mentorship initiatives, EEO records, and budget allocations. These documents provide insight into the organization's culture and operational decision-making.

A limitation of this approach is that it relies primarily on written records rather than direct engagement with employees who understand these documents in context. However, reviewing affirmative action plans, EEO complaints, turnover and absenteeism rates, and employee satisfaction surveys can reveal patterns of inequity. The data can also be used to compare group experiences within the organization. For example, are women leaving at higher rates than men, and what is the financial impact of that turnover? Are Black women disciplined more frequently than other groups for similar infractions? Do absenteeism rates vary significantly among demographic groups? Are job satisfaction levels different based on ethnicity, gender, or job classification? Sufficient archival data can help answer these questions, offering valuable insights for creating a more equitable workplace.

Key Informant Interview (KII). A KII is a qualitative research method that uses structured or semi-structured interviews to gather insights from individuals with extensive knowledge or experience about a specific organization or community. These individuals, termed key informants, are typically chosen for their expertise, leadership positions, or extensive engagement with the organization or community under examination. In our work with city and county transit agencies, the agency's top leader, individual executive team members, the human resource manager, the equal opportunity manager, and a few employees identified as cultural diversity champions were invited to participate as key informants. One employee was a deaf engineer who had visited the HR office several times for accommodations. These interviews, which last 30-40 minutes, explore topics such as the organization's DEI values, existing promotion and retention obstacles, their lived experiences in the organization, and their ideas about improving existing DEI initiatives.

KIIs provide insights that may elude other data-collection techniques. The interviews enable investigators to delve deeply into intricate matters and acquire a holistic comprehension of the subject matter from the perspective of those most acquainted with it. KIIs allow for amassing an elaborate set of information, viewpoints, and judgments about DEI in the organization, obstacles, and successes from individuals well-positioned to be in the know. These interviews commonly delve into themes like organizational values, obstacles to equity and inclusion, challenges in retention and advancement, encounters with discrimination, and tactics to amplify Inclusion Competency. In this way, KIIs serve to unravel the operational and cultural dynamics of an organization, pinpoint hurdles to IEC, and delve into recommendations for reducing resistance.

In a contract with a city government, we discovered that the Spanish-speaking community was expanding rapidly due to the city's location in an agricultural region. One of the diversity champions we interviewed, a Latina woman employed by the city, highlighted the community's Spanish-speaking citizens' contributions to the local economy and shared her frustrations with the city's lack of responsiveness to their needs. She understood that it was particularly important to provide translation services. These interviews offer valuable insights that other data collection methods often overlook or downplay.

Focus Group Interviews. A Focus Group Interview is a qualitative research method that gathers small groups of participants with shared identities, such as employees from the same department, racial identity group, gender, etc., to discuss their experiences and perceptions within an organization. This method is particularly useful for assessing ECDI, as it captures diverse perspectives on workplace culture, policies, and practices, such as DEI initiatives. It is also useful for identifying resistance to DEI. The facilitator guides the discussion using open-ended questions, encouraging participants to share their thoughts, respond to others, and explore different viewpoints. The group dynamic often reveals insights that may not emerge in individual interviews or surveys.

Focus group interviews help organizations understand how different employee groups perceive the organization's culture, identify areas of agreement or conflict, and gather suggestions for improvement. The qualitative data collected provides a rich, detailed understanding of collective experiences, which can inform decision-making, policy development, and organizational strategies. For example, the focus groups we conducted for a transit agency found a disconnect between frontline operators and upper management. Operators expressed frustration with leadership addressing their concerns, while management cited delays in responding to operator complaints caused by resulting from ongoing contract negotiations with the union. The discussions with each group provided valuable insights into organizational decision-making and communication barriers. They also serve as a starting point for trust building and onboarding the workforce to the initiative.

Findings from the focus group and key informant interviews are used to refine DEI strategies, ensuring that initiatives address the real challenges employees face. While focus group findings offer deep insights, they are fraught with the researchers' biases or expectations. This makes the outcomes unreliable for tracking progress and trends over time.

Thematic analysis is subjective, as coding and interpretation depend on the researcher. For this reason, qualitative data are combined with quantitative methods like surveys, which provide numerical tracking of progress over time.

Survey Assessment. The ECDI Assessment Survey is a key tool for evaluating an organization's equity barriers and IEC and tracking progress over time. It efficiently gathers data and measures five critical dimensions: practices, awareness, attitude, knowledge, skills, and practices. The survey consists of 50 Likert scale items, and the results identify the organization's placement along a five-HCDI stage continuum (See Table 1): Conventional (Lowest in equity and inclusion competency organizational culture), Defensive, Ambivalent, Egalitarian, and Equity and Inclusion Competency (Highest in equity and inclusion organizational culture).

The survey is distributed as widely as possible across the organization, capturing responses representing its cultural diversity and segmentation. The results represent one aspect of the organization's current culture, identifying strengths and areas for improvement to inform strategic planning. Ideally, survey participants represent a cross-section of the organization, including different levels, departments, and identity groups, ensuring that the findings accurately reflect the workplace culture.

However, survey data alone cannot fully determine an organization's culture. Combining survey results with interviews and archival data offers a more comprehensive assessment. By integrating quantitative survey data with qualitative insights from interviews and historical records, organizations gain a deeper understanding of their DEI landscape, allowing for targeted, data-driven strategies that drive meaningful and lasting change.

Step 3: Identifying the Current ECDI Stage and Culture

Analyzing both qualitative and quantitative data can be challenging, especially when integrating findings for accurate interpretation. The interviews and equity audits are unstructured and require time-intensive coding and analysis to identify key themes. Quantitative data, by contrast, is more structured and lends itself to statistical analysis. Because qualitative data is nuanced and subjective, and quantitative data is objective and numeric, combining them can be difficult. On their own, neither provides a complete picture. The ECDI framework offers a structured method for integrating both data types to produce a comprehensive and reliable assessment. This section explains the process of converting thematic data into numerical form, aligning it with the same 5-point scale used in the survey. This alignment allows the data sets to be combined for assessing the overall organization's equity and inclusion competency.

Integrating Data for Inclusion-Equity Competency Assessment

A step-by-step guide is beyond the scope of this book. What follows is a general overview. First, the document analysis and each interview data set are coded into positive (e.g., promotes equity), somewhat positive, neutral information (e.g., neither promotes equity or a barrier), somewhat negative, and negative (e.g., equity barrier) shared about the organization, in addition to being thematically organized. The frequency of each code associated with a theme analysis determines how equitable the organization is. A higher frequency of positive themes suggests a higher ECDI culture.

Interview data is further analyzed using a similar 5-point positive to negative ECDI scale. A score closer to one represents low ECDI, and scores closer to or at five represent higher stages. This transformation allows the qualitative data to be integrated with survey results. The more positive the qualitative data themes, the more equity and IEC the organization is assumed to have. The more negative the themes, the lower the stage. A high frequency of neutral themes reflects an organization more in the middle of the path.

The triangulation of the data sources allows for addressing discrepancies among data sources. It is common for the survey results to convey a higher stage of inclusion than the thematic analysis results warrant. Only to the extent that the qualitative results align with the survey results can the stage verification be directly verified. Where there are discrepancies, the qualitative themes are examined more closely. In one organization, the survey scores placed the organization between the Egalitarian and Equity Competence stages. Both interview datasets were represented by higher frequencies of negative themes (e.g., managing cultural diversity and diversity hiring). That warranted lowering the stage to Ambivalent. A closer look at survey data indicated that the survey outcomes were due to it being a predominantly historically majority and included group organization. We were not able to compare group outcomes because there were too few historically marginalized and excluded groups to statistically control for group differences.

Turning Data into Action

The assessment process goes beyond simply interviewing a few employees or distributing a basic questionnaire. CDEI practitioners must use validated assessment tools whenever possible to ensure accurate, high-impact insights. Once the data is collected, the priority is to analyze and interpret the results to identify the current culture stage and develop strategic solutions that drive meaningful organizational change. In summary, a triangulated analysis helps to identify patterns to resolve discrepancies and provide the deeper context needed to determine the equity and inclusion competency more precisely. The resulting numerical dataset is combined with the others and cross-validated. The result provides the organization's CDEI stage. The next step is to summarize and report the results.

Step 4: Create an Assessment Report

An assessment report is a foundational component of a strategic plan. It provides a structured analysis of the organization's current standing and identifies the internal and external conditions that must be addressed to move forward successfully. The following is an outline of a typical assessment report.

1. Executive Summary
   - A brief overview of the assessment findings, highlighting major strengths, challenges, and key opportunities for growth or improvement.
2. Purpose and Scope of the Assessment
   - Clarifies what the assessment set out to examine (e.g., organizational performance, workforce cultural diversity, service equity, operational effectiveness) and how the findings will inform strategic decision-making.
3. Methodology
   - Explains how data was collected (e.g., surveys, focus groups, interviews, document reviews, data analysis) and from whom. Transparency in methods builds trust in the results.
4. Key Findings
   - A detailed presentation of what was discovered. May include: Internal strengths and weaknesses (e.g., leadership capacity, workplace culture, processes)

- External opportunities and threats (e.g., policy changes, demographic shifts, industry trends)
- Equity and inclusion-related disparities (e.g., gaps in representation, promotion access, pay equity)

5. Themes and Patterns
- Synthesizes findings into broader themes, such as communication breakdowns, cultural misalignment, inconsistent accountability, etc.

6. Data Visualizations
- Charts, tables, and graphs to help stakeholders grasp insights quickly and visually.

7. Recommendations
- Initial suggestions or implications drawn from the data that point toward strategic priorities or areas needing intervention.
- The organization creates and shares infographics and summaries describing the results for transparency and workforce updates.

It often also includes:

1. Organizational Profile or Context Section
- The assessment findings are summarized to help explain why strategic change is necessary. This provides a reality check that grounds the plan.

2. SWOT or Environmental Scan Section
- The assessment's internal and external insights feed directly into the SWOT analysis or PESTLE (Political, Economic, Social, Technological, Legal, Environmental) scan.

3. Equity or Cultural Audit Summary (if applicable)
- If the assessment includes findings focused on the performance of cultural diversity initiatives, these may be reported as part of an Equity Assessment or Organizational Climate section, shaping inclusion goals.

4. Strategic Priorities Alignment
- The recommendations or challenges outlined in the assessment are directly linked to the goals, strategies, and action items in

the plan. A strong strategic plan explicitly shows how assessment findings inform goals.

5. Appendix (Optional)

- The full assessment report, or detailed sections of it, are sometimes included in the appendix to preserve transparency and allow for deeper review.

Once the assessment report is completed, the strategic, continuous improvement plan is written.

Step 5: Strategic, Continuous Improvement Report

The strategic planning preparation encompasses several steps to ensure the planning process is well-informed, purposeful, and aligned with the organization's objectives. This starts with utilizing the assessment report to formulate a vision, goals, and objectives.

1. Preparation starts with reviewing the assessment report carefully to understand its fundamental discoveries, deductions, and recommendations. It is imperative to understand the implications for the organization's current stage of ECDI culture delineated in the report, encompassing any identified strengths, weaknesses, opportunities, and threats. The assessment report is meticulously scrutinized to extract pertinent data and insights for high-impact planning. This phase entails understanding the superficial findings, underlying causes, and trends that the data conveys. This provides the perspective needed to frame the organization's culture and a vision for the future state.

2. Upon reviewing the assessment report, the subsequent step involves crafting a vision to steer the strategic planning process. The vision should articulate a lucid, captivating depiction of the organization's aspirations. This vision must be inspiring yet achievable, furnishing a long-term orientation that aligns with the organization's values, mission,

and objectives. The vision should be grounded in the revelations of the assessment report, addressing any identified performance gaps or areas for enhancing cultural diversity, equity and inclusion competency, and removing equity barriers. For instance, if the assessment report underscores a necessity for greater pay equity, clarity in paths to professional mobility, or loss of talent, the organization's vision statement might emphasize evolving into a trailblazer in integrating equity and inclusion into business practices and operations to address these challenges.

3. After formulating a vision, the next step is to define specific strategic goals and objectives to facilitate realizing this vision. The assessment report's findings directly influence the strategic goals and tackle the identified opportunities and challenges. Goals should be SMART—specific, measurable, achievable, relevant, and time-bound—to guarantee they are executable and enable performance tracking over time. For instance, if the report pinpoints a gap in retaining historically marginalized and excluded group managers, a strategic goal could be to design, develop, and implement a plan with specific actions to increase their retention within the next two years.

4. In addition to setting goals, pinpointing key priorities and focus areas is crucial. This step involves ascertaining which facets of the organization's operations or processes necessitate the most attention based on the assessment report. Prioritization ensures that the organization's resources are allocated effectively and that action planning concentrates on areas that will yield the most significant impact. This may include focusing on areas such as enhancing professional development or addressing salary inequities.

5. Once priorities are established, it is vital to devise a strategic plan that delineates the specific actions and initiatives that will be undertaken to accomplish the culture change goals. This plan should be comprehensive and encompass timelines, responsible parties, and requisite resources. The strategic plan should also contemplate potential risks and how they will be addressed. It is crucial to ascertain that

the plan is pragmatic and considers the organization's capacity and constraints. This involves considering financial resources, personnel, and organizational culture.

6. Monitoring and ongoing evaluation are also integral to the strategic planning process. Establishing key performance indicators (KPIs) predicated on the strategic goals enables the organization to gauge progress and make adaptations as necessary. Regularly assessing these KPIs and evaluating progress against the strategic plan ensures that the organization remains on course to achieve its vision. It also permits the identification of any emerging challenges or opportunities that may necessitate a shift in strategy.

7. Lastly, remaining flexible and adaptable throughout the strategic planning process is crucial. The environment in which organizations operate can evolve swiftly, and the capability to adapt the strategic plan to new circumstances is vital for long-term success. This adaptability should be integrated into the strategic planning process, allowing for periodic reviews and updates to the plan when necessary.

By adhering to these five steps, an organization can prepare for strategic, continuous improvement planning, which is informed by a thorough assessment, guided by a clear vision, and focused on attaining meaningful and sustainable outcomes. This approach ensures that strategic planning is not merely a theoretical exercise but a pragmatic and dynamic process that propels the organization forward. Given the importance of evaluating the assessment report, more clarity about how to do that systematically is warranted.

Reviewing the Assessment Report

A structured and detailed approach is essential to review an assessment report in preparation for designing and developing an ECDI initiative. This will ensure that the initiative is well-informed, effective, and tailored to the organization's specific needs, context, and developmental stage.

First, it is crucial to understand the scope and purpose of the assessment report. This involves clarifying the gaps uncovered by the assessment and their workforce impact, especially with respect to employee and management productivity and customer satisfaction. Next, the key findings are examined, such as workplace demographics and competency gaps identified across various levels of the organization (e.g., leadership, middle management, and staff).

Qualitative data from the interviews, focus groups, and archival analyses are reviewed to gain a deeper understanding of workplace culture, perceived equity barriers, and areas needing improvement. Identifying significant trends or patterns that emerge from the survey data, such as the equity and inclusion competency of the organization and different departments, is essential. It is also important to look for disparities or gaps in the data, such as inequities in disciplinary actions or professional development. Where cultural diversity may be concentrated on the organizational chart is also important to uncover. For example, analyzing the degree to which historically marginalized and excluded groups are concentrated in the lower-level jobs compared to the executive and middle management levels.

The next step is to evaluate the report's recommendations. This involves assessing whether the recommendations are feasible given the organization's resources, current demands, and resistance to change to determine if the recommendations are realistic and actionable. Ensuring the recommendations align with the organization's broader goals and values is crucial, as they should support its mission and strategic priorities. It is also essential to consider which recommendations should be prioritized based on the assessment findings, focusing on high-impact areas that significantly improve ECDI outcomes. Attempting to increase cultural diversity in leadership when there is a hiring freeze will be daunting without a policy change. Consider the high cost of obtaining a Master of Library Science (MLS) degree to compete for a librarian job. This requirement for many library positions has created a barrier to hiring candidates from historically marginalized and excluded group populations, yet it is questionable that a degree is necessary. Financial barriers, lack of awareness that the profession exists, underrepresentation, systemic biases in the application process, and other cultural and social barriers contribute to inequities in job opportunity access.

Identifying data gaps and additional needs is another key aspect of the review process. It is necessary to determine the critical areas the report needs to cover. For instance, if the report lacks data on certain demographics, it may not fully represent the organization's cultural diversity. Determining if additional research or data collection is needed to gain a more comprehensive understanding of the ECDI landscape within the organization may also be necessary. A city government in Colorado realized after an assessment that it had a growing population of Spanish-speaking citizens due to its location in an agricultural region. Yet, few of them worked for the city. Their voices were not in the data, yet their needs were growing, as determined by the number of Spanish-speaking citizens seeking city services.

Engaging stakeholders to gain insights and feedback is also essential. This includes involving internal stakeholders such as middle managers and the leadership, steering committee members, human resource management, and employee resource groups in discussions to gain diverse perspectives on the findings and recommendations. Consulting with external ECDI experts or facilitators can provide an unbiased view of the assessment findings and help interpret complex data. Sharing the results in focus groups with staff and, when possible, customers will be helpful.

Interpreting the findings in the context of the organization's culture, history, and external environment is crucial.

It is important to understand how the organization's culture may influence implementing the ECDI initiative and outcomes and consider historical or cultural factors that may impact diversity, equity, and inclusion efforts. Comparing the findings to industry norms and benchmarks can help understand where the organization stands in relation to its peers. Still, it is more critical to compare progress toward becoming more culturally inclusive and equitable based on internal data, data indicating that the organization is shifting towards greater stages of inclusion and equity competency.

Writing the Strategic Plan Document

Once a needs assessment is completed, a vision statement is created, key stakeholders are engaged, core values and principles are defined, and the future state has been envisioned, the next step is to organize the information in a written plan. The plan includes the following:

1. Executive summary
2. Organizational profile
3. Environmental scan
4. Strategic objectives and goals
5. Change management strategy
6. Implementation plan
7. Communication plan
8. Performance monitoring plan
9. Risk management plan
10. Appendices

Each is discussed below.

Executive Summary

An executive summary of the culture change strategic plan overviews the plan's purpose, key goals, strategies, and expected outcomes. It is limited to one to two pages for conciseness and is written to compel stakeholder engagement, such as executives, employees, and partners. The following outlines how to craft an effective executive summary:

1. <u>Start with a Strong Opening Statement.</u> Clearly define the purpose of the culture change initiative. For example, "This strategic plan outlines our approach to fostering an inclusive, equitable, and high-performing workplace culture that aligns with our core values and business objectives."

2. <u>Outline the Need for Change.</u> Briefly describe why culture change is necessary. Summarize the findings in the assessment report, adding narratives from participant comments that bolster the need for change. For example, "The assessment report indicates that the current organizational culture falls short of creating an equitable workplace, especially for the front-line workers."

3. <u>Define the Vision & Goals.</u> Restate the list of culture change goals. For example:

   a. A culture in which every individual feels a sense of belonging, equity is the norm, and inclusion competency drives innovation and success.

   b. An equitable workplace where barriers are broken, voices are heard, and every team member has a pathway to thrive.

   c. A future where inclusion and equity are not initiatives but fundamental values that define our organization's success.

4. <u>Summarize the Key Strategies.</u> This section highlights the core initiatives that will drive change. For example:

   a. Leadership training and accountability frameworks.

   b. Revised policies, procedures, and practices to improve equity.

   c. Workforce Inclusion-Equity competency training completion.

5. <u>Mention the Expected Impact & Metrics for Success.</u> State how the culture shift will benefit employees and the organization. Identify key performance indicators (KPIs) such as:

   a. Employee engagement scores.

   b. Inclusion-Equity Competency training completion.

   c. Employee complaints.

   d. Retention and turnover rates.

6. <u>Call to Action.</u> This section encourages leadership and stakeholders to champion the change. For example, "It is imperative that all leaders and employees take an active role in supporting the transformation needed to enhance cultural diversity and Inclusion-Equity Competency needed to drive our organization's success."

In summary, the executive summary is an overview of the purpose, key goals, strategies, and expected outcomes should the needed change be achieved. Keep the tone inspirational and forward-looking. Align language with organizational values and priorities.

Organizational Profile

The organizational profile* provides a snapshot of the organization, setting the context for the change report. It is a clear, concise, and focused summary of the key elements that influence the organization's culture. Below is a structured approach to writing an effective organizational profile:

1. Organization overview
a. Name of the organization
b. Industry/Sector
c. The office location(s) (Headquarters, regional offices, global presence)
d. The organization was founded in 2003.

Example: APECK Corporation is a leading technology firm specializing in cloud-based learning management solutions. Headquartered in San Francisco, the company operates in over fifteen countries, serving enterprise and mid-market clients.

2. Mission, Vision, and Core Values

The organization's purpose is clearly stated, along with a description of the long-term aspirations and core values that guide the culture and decision-making.

Example: APECK's mission is to empower businesses with innovative technology solutions that enhance learning management efficiency and high-impact collaboration tools. We envision a future where technology drives sustainable growth and equitable access to digital tools. Our core values include transparency, inclusion, equity, innovation, and customer-centered solutions.

3. Organizational Structure

Describe the governance structure.

Example: APECK operates under a matrix structure, with cross-functional teams driving key initiatives. The executive leadership team includes the CEO, CFO, CTO, Chief Diversity Officer, and a steering committee that oversees culture transformation efforts.

4. Workforce Demographics & Culture Snapshot

a. List the number of employees and workforce composition.

b. Provide the cultural diversity metrics.

c. List the organization's current cultural strengths and challenges.

Example: With 5,000 employees worldwide, APECK Corporation maintains a diverse workforce, with 45% of employees identifying as racially White and 20% as Asian, 22% Latino/Hispanic,10% African American, and 3% Unknown. Males outnumber women by two to one. One percent identify as LGBTQIA+ and half a percent as persons who are differently abled. While the organization enjoys a collaborative workforce, recent employee surveys indicate a need for greater psychological safety, equity, and inclusion competency among the leadership. The latter needs to be addressed to increase innovation.

5. Key Business Challenges & Market Position

This section summarizes the industry trends affecting the organization.

Example: The Learning Management System (LMS) industry is experiencing significant growth, driven by technological advancements and evolving educational needs. As a leader in the learning technology space, APECK Corporation faces increasing competition from emerging artificial intelligence (AI) technologies, startups with AI solutions, and evolving customer expectations for ethical AI solutions. To remain competitive, we must foster a culture of agility, continuous learning, and innovation that requires harnessing our culturally diverse talent.

6. Why Culture Change is Necessary

The need for culture change is linked to strategic business goals in this section. Triggers, such as mergers, employee feedback, compliance issues, and leadership changes, are described.

Example: In response to shifting workforce talent needs and our commitment to DEI, APECK Corporation is embarking on a multi-year culture transformation initiative. This will enhance talent management, strengthen leadership accountability, and align our culture with long-term business goals. The organization is currently navigating significant headwinds, including shifts in the competitive landscape and mounting pressures to adapt to evolving market demands. Emerging competitors, digital disruption, and changing customer expectations require a more agile and innovative approach to remain relevant. Internally, rising turnover rates and challenges in retaining top talent signal a need to reassess organizational culture, engagement strategies, and leadership alignment. These dynamics underscore the urgency for transformative change to ensure long-term sustainability and growth.

7. Call to Action for Stakeholders

Provide brief statement on leadership commitment and how stakeholders can contribute to culture change.

Example: We invite employees, leaders, and partners to actively engage in this cultural transformation, ensuring that our organization remains a leader in innovation and equity.

The organizational profile provides context and highlights the need for transformation, serving as the foundation for the Strategic Culture Change Report.

8. Environmental Scan. The environmental scan summary formulating a strategic culture change plan. This process involves a

comprehensive assessment of both internal and external factors that influence an organization's culture, providing a foundation for informed decision-making and effective strategy development.

The summary includes:

a. Internal Environment Analysis. The organization's readiness for change, workforce's prevailing values, beliefs, and behaviors learned from the assessment, communication channels, employee resistance, and leadership commitment are included in the summary.

b. External Environment Analysis. This section of the summary identifies industry trends that may necessitate cultural shifts, such as technological advancements and increased competition.

c. Regulatory and Legal Factors. This summary covers laws and regulations that impact organizational practices and culture.

d. Societal and Cultural Norms. Understand societal expectations and cultural norms that influence organizational behavior and employee expectations, such as the impact of a majority Christian population on politics and public sentiment.

e. Competitive Landscape. Analyze competitors' cultures and practices to identify areas for improvement or differentiation.

9. SWOT Analysis

This section summarizes the organization's internal cultural strengths, such as an existing cultural diversity management strategy, that can be leveraged during the change process. Any weaknesses are included, such as a lack of Inclusion-Equity Competency needed to fully realize the potential of the organization's existing cultural diversity. Summarize the external opportunities that align with the desired cultural direction, such as the proliferation of AI technologies and solutions. Acknowledge external challenges, or threat, that could impede cultural transformation efforts, such as competitors entering the AI solution marker.

10. PEST Analysis.

The PEST acronym stands for Political, Economic, Social, and Technological factors. The summary includes the political and regulatory factors that affect the culture change, such as anti-DEI legislation that may indirectly impact workforce and leadership commitment. Economic conditions that influence resource availability, such as demographic shifts and societal trends that impact workplace dynamics, and details about how AI technological changes require cultural adaptations, such as embracing innovative technologies and continuous learning.

The environmental scan summary encompasses the above components and describes the potential impact on the culture change initiative. It also provides insight into the organization's readiness for change.

Craft the Mission and Vision Statement

This section explains how to craft the mission and vision statement that support the plan's development. It outlines the mission statement section that defines the purpose, core values, impact, and actionable commitments, with a sample provided. Crafting the vision statement section focuses on articulating a clear, aspirational future state that motivates stakeholders and guides long-term direction. It emphasizes the importance of stakeholder involvement, mindset shifts, and using assessment data to identify and address barriers to equity. The historical context is included to highlight the legacy of exclusion and its relevance to current practices. Finally, the section discusses how to embed and communicate the vision throughout the organization to guide decisions, promote accountability, and sustain the ECDI initiative.

Mission Statement: Defining Purpose and Commitment

Crafting a clear, inspiring, and action-oriented mission statement is a foundational step in shaping an ECDI culture. It should reflect the organization's commitment to creating a workplace where all individuals feel included, treated fairly, and valued regardless of job role or position. The mission must also address the importance of attending to the perceptions and needs of those at the lower levels of the organization, who often most significantly experience inequities and hold valuable insights for driving change.

The mission statement should also reflect how ECDI principles are embedded in policies, procedures, and practices. Developing the statement involves addressing four key components:

1. Define the Purpose – Why is an ECDI culture essential to your organization?

2. State Core Values – What values guide the commitment to inclusion, equity, and cultural diversity?

3. Clarify the Impact – How will an ECDI culture benefit the workforce, stakeholders, and broader community?

4. Identify Actionable Commitments – What concrete steps will the organization take to fulfill this mission?

Sample Mission Statement:

APECX's mission is to cultivate a culture in which each employee can thrive, regardless of job role, title, or position. We are committed to fostering a workplace that embraces diverse perspectives and removes barriers to equity. Through continuous education, accountability, and engagement, we aim to build a culture where diversity, equity, and inclusion drive meaningful change and organizational success.

Vision Statement: Painting the Future State

After establishing the mission, a clear and compelling ECDI vision statement articulates the desired future state that the organization aspires to achieve. It should be concise, aspirational, values-driven, and future-oriented—designed to inspire stakeholders and guide long-term strategy. Crafting the vision statement is a structured process that includes:

1. Clarifying Purpose – Reinforce why the ECDI transformation is critical.

2. Identifying Core Values – Anchor the vision in values that guide inclusive-equity competence growth.

3. Describing the Future Culture – Define the envisioned culture (e.g., where equity is embedded in operations and barriers are removed).

4. Creating Actionable Goals – Go beyond ideals to outline realistic, motivating steps.

5. Writing a Memorable Statement – Make it short, powerful, and easy to communicate.

Sample Vision Statements:

- A culture in which each individual member feels a sense of belonging, equity is the norm, and an ECDI culture drives innovation and success.
- An equitable workplace where barriers are broken, voices are heard, and each team member has a pathway to thrive.
- A future where inclusion and equity are not initiatives but core values that define our success.

Making It Real: Stakeholder Engagement and Strategy Integration

Involving key stakeholders in drafting and refining both the mission and vision ensures alignment and buy-in. Reimagining the culture requires a shift in mindset—especially from leadership—to recognize that current systems may reinforce bias and underutilize talent. Assessment data are used to illustrate how current assumptions and practices may hinder fairness, innovation, and productivity.

The ECDI strategic plan supports this culture shift by:

- Educating staff on the history of organizational inequities.
- Highlighting systemic patterns of exclusion (e.g., gender discrimination, racial property exclusion, and academic barriers).

- Encouraging leaders to acknowledge past harms and take responsibility for inclusive practices moving forward.

Communicating and Using the Vision

Once finalized, the vision must be embedded in all aspects of the ECDI initiative. It should be communicated clearly and frequently through strategic plans, policy documents, training programs, and internal communications. Leaders and managers should champion the vision consistently, using it to:

- Guide decision-making
- Resolving conflicts or disagreements are the organization's goal and objectives
- Evaluate progress
- Align strategies with core values

The vision serves as a guiding star, keeping the organization focused on creating a future grounded in inclusion, equity, and shared success.

By following this process, organizations can craft a compelling vision and vision statement that provides a clear, inspirational direction for the initiative, serving to drive meaningful and sustainable change toward a more culturally diverse, equitable, and inclusive future.

Identifying the Priorities, Goals, and Metrics

The strategic plan serves as a roadmap for achieving desired outcomes and advancing the organization's ECDI goals. Identifying key priorities and focus areas for an ECDI initiative involves revisiting the organization's specific needs, challenges, and opportunities outlined in the assessment report. Goals are then developed to address each area. This process ensures the initiative is targeted, effective, and aligned with the organization's mission and vision. Each goal should be SMART: specific, measurable, achievable, relevant, and time-bound. For example, if the organization's broad objective is to enhance innovation and creativity by incorporating cultural diversity into talent management, a strategic goal might be to increase cultural diversity in teams based on research linking diversity to improved innovation. A related subgoal could be to offer training in culturally diverse team building and communication skills to help teams fully leverage their differences.

To improve employee retention, a goal might be to enhance a sense of fairness by identifying and removing barriers to equity. A subgoal will likely be to provide training on managing retention by improving work-life balance and increasing pay inequity. Aligning ECDI initiative goals with organizational objectives ensures that the initiative is integrated into the organization's overall strategy and that efforts are focused on areas that will drive meaningful change.

With strategic goals defined, the next step is to prioritize key focus areas for the initiative based on their feasibility and potential for shifting the organization to higher stages. Consider which areas will significantly impact achieving the strategic goals and advancing ECDI within the organization. Rank the goals regarding the potential for positive change, the number of employees or stakeholders affected, and alignment with the initiative's stated values and objectives. This feasibility analysis also considers the resources required to address each focus area, including time, budget, human resources, and potential challenges or barriers. Focus areas that are high-impact and highly feasible should be prioritized for immediate action. In contrast, areas with lower impact or feasibility are included later in the longer-term cultural shift strategy.

The full report is shared with leadership and upper management and summarized for presentation to the entire organization. Identifying the organization's current stage of ECDI culture is followed by developing a robust cultural change plan.

Step 6: Develop a Continuous Improvement Plan

Continuous improvement planning introduces a regular cycle of reflection, evaluation, and adjustment that allows the organization to assess what's working, what's not, and why. It helps leaders gather feedback, track incremental changes, and make data-informed decisions to overcome resistance, address emerging challenges, and build trust across all levels. Without this dual approach, a strategic plan may remain aspirational but unimplemented, while continuous improvement alone may lack direction and alignment with broader organizational goals. Together, they create a dynamic system: the strategic plan sets the vision and structures for accountability, while continuous improvement ensures persistent, iterative action that chips away at structural inequities over time. In organizations with deep-rooted barriers to inclusion, this combination is critical because it balances ambitious goals with realistic, ongoing action. This builds credibility, fosters engagement, and create the conditions for sustainable cultural change.

Creating a continuous improvement plan begins by carefully reviewing the strategic plan to identify its key goals, objectives, and success measures. From these, determine which outcomes require continuous tracking and improvement. Focus on areas where implementation will be complex, progress may be uneven, or barriers may arise. Common barriers include professional development for mobility within the organizations and pay inequities. Next, for each strategic goal, break it down into smaller, measurable milestones or performance indicators that can be monitored on an ongoing basis. This step transforms broad strategic intentions into short-term targets that teams can realistically achieve and assess. Creating mentorship programs for professional development and analyzing payroll data to identify inequities are examples.

Consider this more elaborate example. Improving supervisor and manager inclusion competency in equitable talent management will be implemented for all managers within four months, aiming for 95%

completion and a 30% increase in equity competency scores, as measured by pre- and post-training assessments. To reinforce accountability, equity and inclusion competency should be incorporated into annual manager performance evaluations in the next review cycle, ensuring that 100% of managers are evaluated on this competency. Furthermore, quarterly peer learning groups for managers should be established to foster shared problem-solving, with each session generating documented action plans to address ongoing barriers.

Monitoring and reporting progress is essential to sustaining momentum. An equity progress scorecard, including baseline and target metrics for talent management, should be developed within 60 days and presented quarterly to executive leadership. Progress toward reducing disparities should also be tracked.

The continuous improvement report needs to include a cycle of review and feedback by establishing clear timelines for evaluating progress, which can be quarterly, monthly, or tied to specific project phases. Identify who is responsible for monitoring each metric, gathering feedback, and recommending adjustments. This ensures accountability and keeps momentum moving forward. Importantly, the continuous improvement plan needs to include mechanisms for gathering input from stakeholders throughout the organization. This might involve regular surveys, focus groups, team debriefs, or informal check-ins to assess what's working, what barriers persist, and where adjustments are needed.

Each review cycle should lead to specific recommendations for adjustments or next steps, which are then integrated back into operations. Over time, these iterative improvements help close gaps between the organization's current state and its strategic goals. Finally, the continuous improvement plan should be a living document, designed to evolve as new challenges, opportunities, or insights emerge. By linking the strategic plan's long-term vision with this flexible, action-oriented process, the practitioner, committee, and leadership can ensure that progress remains steady, responsive, and aligned with the organization's mission.

Step 7: Create a Communication Plan

Communication plays a pivotal role in strategic planning. Communicating the vision, goals, and strategic plan to all stakeholders, encompassing employees, management, and external partners, is imperative. Clear communication ensures that everyone is on the same page and understands their role in executing the strategic plan. It also fosters a sense of ownership and dedication across the workforce to the organization's future direction. Engaging stakeholders in the planning process can also result in valuable feedback and insights, aiding in refining and fortifying the strategic plan.

An organizational change communication plan guides the dissemination of information during periods of transformation within an organization. Its primary purpose is to ensure that all stakeholders, including employees, managers, leadership, and relevant external partners, are informed, engaged, and aligned with the change initiatives. The key components include the change initiative's vision statement and objectives, the list of stakeholders, and the impact of the change on each stakeholder group. Use the information to develop a tailored message before releasing the communications.

The plan identifies communication channels and describes tactics. It also describes a timeline and frequency for communications. The designated communicators are listed, and any required tools and information, along with training, are listed.

Step 8: Create an Implementation Plan

With the culture change strategy now documented, the next step is to develop a structured implementation plan to systematically integrate inclusion and equity practices into the organization's culture, policies, and operations. To implement these strategies and tactics effectively, it is important to develop a detailed plan including specific actions, timelines, responsible parties, and required resources. The plan should be communicated clearly to all employees, and progress should be monitored regularly to ensure alignment with the organization's ECDI goals.

Assign Responsibilities and Establish Accountability

Assign responsibilities and establish accountability for each objective, strategy, and tactic in the strategic plan. Identify who within the organization will lead and oversee each component, including specific tasks and actions. Roles should be designated across all levels, from senior leadership to individual employees and diversity committees. This ensures everyone understands what is expected in advancing the ECDI initiative. This clarity promotes ownership, alignment, and commitment throughout the organization.

Particular attention should be given to middle management, who often serve as the gatekeepers of organizational culture. While leadership may change over time, middle managers typically remain in their roles longer and have lasting influence. Their involvement is essential as they are best positioned to bridge the gap between senior leadership and frontline staff. A targeted strategy is needed to engage middle managers, build their sense of ownership, and align their efforts with the organization's equity goals. Their active participation is critical to the long-term success of any ECDI initiative.

The first step is to ensure that middle managers understand the importance of the ECDI initiative and how it aligns with the organization's overall mission and values. This can be achieved through clear communication from senior leadership, explaining how creating an ECDI culture can offer a competitive edge essential for creating a thriving, innovative, and productive workplace. Providing middle managers with data, case studies, and research that show the positive impacts of ECDI efforts on employee satisfaction, productivity, and business outcomes can help get their buy-in. When middle managers understand the business case for diversity and inclusion and what's in it for them to support the initiative, they are more likely to take it on as part of their responsibility to lead these efforts.

Training and development programs focused on increasing IEC are another way to engage middle management. These programs should go beyond the basics of IEC training and delve into practical strategies for managing diverse teams, addressing unconscious bias, identifying sources of and barriers to equity, and fostering an inclusive workplace. Offering workshops, seminars, and coaching sessions can equip middle managers with the skills and knowledge they need to implement ECDI within their departments. These training programs should also emphasize the role of managers in creating a culture of inclusion, making it clear that their actions and behaviors set the tone for their teams. Managers often identify the areas in which they need additional training while completing these training modules. Use the information to provide them with the additional training as quickly as possible. Include them in the training design and development as much as possible.

Accountability is a key component in getting middle management involved. ECDI-related goals and metrics can be incorporated into performance evaluations to ensure they actively contribute to the initiative. This could include tracking their efforts to promote diverse hiring practices, support employee resource groups, or implement policies that foster equity. Tying contributions to ECDI efforts to performance appraisals and rewards, middle managers will understand that these initiatives are not optional but a core part of their leadership responsibilities.

Creating a sense of ownership among middle managers is essential and can be done by involving representatives in the planning and decision-making process of the ECDI initiative. When middle managers have a say in how the initiative is designed and rolled out, especially as it relates directly to them, they are more likely to feel invested in its success. This could involve forming committees or task forces that include middle management representatives, allowing them to voice their ideas and concerns. Such collaboration also helps tailor the initiative to meet different departments' specific needs and challenges, ensuring it is more effective and sustainable.

To foster engagement, it is essential to provide middle managers with the necessary resources and support. This could include tools such as templates, checklists, guidelines, or access to external expertise to help them implement ECDI effectively. Senior leadership should also clarify that middle managers have the organization's backing in their efforts, providing regular check-ins and opportunities for feedback to address any challenges they might encounter. Encouraging managers to share best practices and successes across departments can actively create a support network and motivate others to promote diversity, equity, and inclusion.

Recognition and celebration of middle managers' efforts to implement ECDI further reinforce their involvement. Publicly acknowledging their contributions, whether through internal communications, awards, or during company meetings, helps validate their work and encourages continued participation. This also signals to others in the organization that ECDI efforts are valued and rewarded at all levels of management.

Lastly, it is vital to encourage middle managers to serve as change agents within their teams. When they feel confident in their ability to influence positive change, they are more likely to take proactive steps in addressing equity and inclusion barriers. Providing them with opportunities to mentor others, complete ECDI-related actions and goals, and contribute to the broader organizational strategy helps build their capacity as leaders in this area. In doing so, middle managers become integral to driving cultural change within the organization, ensuring that the ECDI initiative is implemented and embraced throughout the company. Treating them as partners instead of a source of resistance will increase the chances of the change initiative's success. One manager who had been somewhat oppositional during the kickoff meeting became an active champion of the work after completing a managing for racial equity training. Their influence was significant enough to help us secure broader access to participants for our sessions.

It is also important to establish accountability mechanisms, such as regular progress reports, performance reviews, and check-ins, to monitor progress and ensure that the strategic plan stays on track. Assigning a dedicated ECDI leader and equity and inclusion competency committee members to oversee the initiative can help maintain focus and momentum.

Allocate Resources and Define a Budget

An ECDI initiative's strategic plan requires adequate financial, human, and technological resources. Define the budget and allocate the resources necessary to implement the strategies and tactics effectively. Consider the costs associated with each tactic, such as training programs, recruitment efforts, technology upgrades, or external consultants. Ensure that the budget aligns with the priorities of the ECDI initiative and that sufficient resources are allocated to high-impact areas.

In addition to financial resources, consider the human resources needed, such as hiring additional staff or dedicating existing personnel to the ECDI initiative. Identify any technological resources required, such as software for tracking diversity metrics or online platforms for training and engagement. Protect the resources. An organizational change initiative requires at least five years of resource commitment. Outline a realistic budget that balances cost-effectiveness with the reality of economic turbulence over time (e.g., increased costs and budget restriction changes).

Create a Detailed Implementation Timeline

A detailed implementation timeline is essential to guide the execution of the strategic plan and ensure that all actions are completed within the set timeframe. Develop a timeline that outlines when each tactic will be implemented and the goal will be completed, considering the priorities and sequencing of actions. The timeline should include specific milestones and deadlines for each objective, strategy, and tactic, providing a clear roadmap for achieving the desired outcomes. It is important to be realistic in setting timelines, considering any potential challenges or barriers that may arise. Building flexibility into the timeline is also crucial to accommodate unforeseen circumstances or adjustments that may be needed as the initiative progresses. Regularly reviewing and updating the timeline helps ensure that the strategic plan remains relevant and effective.

Develop Metrics and Key Performance Indicators

As indicated, it is essential to develop metrics and KPIs to evaluate the success of the ECDI initiative and measure progress toward the strategic goals. Metrics and KPIs provide quantifiable measures that can be used to assess the effectiveness of the strategies and tactics and track progress over time. Identify the key metrics and KPIs for each objective. For example, metrics might include the percentage increase in cultural diversity in middle management and leadership roles, the number of employees completing IEC training, or employee satisfaction scores related to the ECDI initiative. Of course, KPIs should be closely aligned with the objectives and clearly indicate progress and success. A well-defined set of metrics and KPIs provides clarity, accountability, and a means to track the impact of the efforts over time. Here is a detailed approach to developing these metrics and KPIs.

Specific metrics and KPIs should be developed that align with the organization's ECDI objectives. These metrics should be quantitative and qualitative to assess progress and impact comprehensively. For example, workforce cultural diversity metrics might include the percentage of employees from different demographic groups across various organizational levels and functions, diversity in recruitment and hiring practices, and cultural diversity in leadership representation.

ECDI metrics could involve comparing compensation levels across different demographic groups in similar roles to identify pay gaps, promotion rates for different demographic groups, and equitable access to development opportunities. Inclusion and employee experience metrics might include an inclusion index from employee survey scores, employee engagement scores broken down by demographic groups, and employee perceptions of psychological safety.

Retention and turnover metrics are useful for analyzing turnover rates by demographic group to identify patterns or disparities and track retention rates for diverse employees over time, particularly in critical or leadership roles. Leadership and accountability metrics might include the number of leaders who have completed EIC training and are actively involved in the initiative and the inclusion of the goals in performance reviews and leadership accountability metrics. Program and initiative effectiveness metrics are suitable for measuring training completion rates, evaluating the impact of DEI programs on participants, and gathering qualitative feedback from employees on the effectiveness and relevance of Implementing DEI.

It is essential that metrics clearly define what is being measured and why it is important, be quantifiable or assessed qualitatively with clear criteria, set realistic and attainable targets that consider the organization's resources and context, align with the organization's strategic DEI goals and objectives, and establish a timeframe for achieving the targets to ensure timely progress and accountability.

The baseline data that establishes the organization's current culture stage is necessary for effectively implementing the metrics and KPIs. The results from historical data concerning the key focus areas provide a starting point for measuring progress. Once baseline data is established, specific targets are set for each metric or KPI. For example, if recruitment policies and procedures include equity barriers, a target increases a sense of fairness in the recruitment process by forty percent in six months.

Robust data collection and reporting processes are needed to track and measure metrics and KPIs effectively. This includes defining data sources, ensuring data accuracy and consistency, automating data collection processes to reduce manual effort and increase efficiency, and developing a reporting schedule to regularly review progress against targets, such as monthly, quarterly, or annual reports to key stakeholders. Communicating the selected metrics and KPIs across the organization is also crucial to ensure transparency and buy-in. Sharing the metrics and KPIs with employees, managers, and leaders through various communication channels, such as town hall meetings, internal newsletters, and intranet portals, helps clarify how these metrics align with the organization's DEI goals and each employee's role in achieving them.

Continuous monitoring of progress against the ECDI metrics and KPIs is essential to assess the effectiveness of the DEI strategic plan. The data collected should be used to identify trends, successes, and areas needing improvement. If certain metrics are not meeting targets, it is important to analyze the underlying reasons and adjust strategies or tactics accordingly. Flexibility is crucial to adapt to changing circumstances or new insights. Finally, metrics and KPIs should be used to drive continuous improvement in the ECDI efforts. Regularly reviewing and analyzing the data helps to understand the impact of Implementing the initiative and identify opportunities for the most significant impact. Sharing successes and learnings across the organization fosters a culture of continuous improvement and encourages ongoing commitment to a culture of inclusive equity.

Regularly tracking and analyzing these metrics and KPIs allows the organization to assess the impact of the ECDI initiative, identify areas for improvement, and make data-driven decisions to refine and enhance the strategic plan. By following this structured approach, an organization can develop robust metrics and KPIs for its DEI strategic plan. This enables it to measure progress effectively, demonstrate accountability, and make data-driven decisions to achieve its DEI goals.

Recognizing Readiness for Change

Once the data-driven strategic plan report is developed, the first order of business is to present it to the leadership and management team members. Their feedback will help determine if they are ready to move forward with a strategic plan. An organization's readiness for change, especially following an assessment report that indicates the need for a cultural shift, depends on several factors determining its capacity and willingness to implement a strategic plan for transforming the culture. An assessment report recommending cultural change typically suggests that the current organizational practices, values, and behaviors are not fully inclusive and equitable, such as outdated policies and procedures, more punitive remediation for African Americans, and gender pay inequity.

Getting clear about leadership and management's commitment and support for the initiative is critical for assessing an organization's readiness for change. Leaders must be fully engaged in the change process, understand why the shift is necessary, recognize its benefits for the organization, and actively demonstrate their support for the initiative. Their involvement includes partnering with the ECDI practitioner to set a clear vision, communicating the benefits of the shift to the larger organization, fostering support from middle management, and modeling the desired behaviors supporting change. A high level of engagement from leaders often correlates with greater organizational readiness for change. If they balk at committing to any of these actions on their part, that offers insight into how to proceed.

Additionally, readiness is shaped by how well employees and stakeholders understand the need for change. Awareness of the issues highlighted in the assessment report, the reason for shifting the culture, and why change needs to occur now is essential for building a sense of urgency and ensuring employees are on board with adopting new behaviors and attitudes. Without this understanding, the organization may face resistance or apathy, undermining the change efforts.

The existing organizational culture and its history with change also impact readiness. Organizations with a culture that is adaptable, open to new ideas, and supportive of continuous improvement tend to be more prepared and open for change. In contrast, organizations with a history of resistance to change, rigid hierarchies, or lack of innovation may create significant challenges in shifting the culture. Understanding the current culture is vital for developing a change strategy that addresses potential barriers.

Employee engagement is another critical factor in readiness for change. When employees are involved in shaping the new culture and feel that their input is valued, they are more likely to support the change. Readiness for change is stronger when there is broad involvement across various levels and functions within the organization. This inclusive approach ensures diverse perspectives are considered, fosters a sense of ownership, and reduces resistance. Training and workshops are effective ways to engage employees, especially when the need for change is clearly communicated, participants have time to ask questions, and they are given at least one actionable step to support the initiative.

In a mandatory racial equity training for frontline workers, our training covered the historical context of social justice, oppression, and inequities, the lingering effects of past inequities on current workplace dynamics, and how these issues impact productivity. The training also introduced a practical technique for identifying inequities, such as recognizing off-color jokes, unconscious bias in hiring (e.g., hiring people who look like ourselves), and understanding how equity issues affect health and wellness and undermine productive teamwork. Our training received an average approval rating of 86% based on post-training evaluations, even during the height of the anti-DEI movement. The technique participants learned equipped them to help reduce workplace inequities and prepared them for more advanced training. Most notably, they actively promoted the training to colleagues who had not yet attended.

The presence of resources and the capability to navigate change are pivotal facets of preparedness. Organizations need ample financial resources, time, staff, and proficiency to take on the recommendations in the assessment report. The necessary resources must be implemented, including a project management plan and a communication plan. Project management and support mechanisms are equally crucial to aid employees in acclimating to fresh cultural standards. Even endeavors for change driven by strong desire and good intentions can falter without adequate resources.

Understanding and anticipating potential resistance is also part of an organization's readiness for change. Knowing who might resist the cultural shift, the reasons for their resistance, and how to address their concerns are crucial steps in the change process. Organizations that anticipate and proactively prepare for and address resistance through targeted communication, education workshops, training, and engagement efforts are better prepared for successful change implementation.

Furthermore, having mechanisms to measure progress and gather feedback is essential for readiness. Organizations need to establish clear metrics for success and processes to monitor the cultural shift's effectiveness. Regular feedback allows for necessary adjustments and keeps the change process on track, increasing the likelihood of success.

Lastly, employees' and leaders' emotional and psychological readiness is a significant factor. Cultural change can be challenging and require people to confront deeply held beliefs or alter long-standing behaviors. Leaders ready for change must work with the practitioner to assess the emotional and psychological climate and provide support, such as coaching, counseling, or team-building activities, to help employees navigate the transition.

Risk management is a pivotal element of organizational change, encompassing the identification, evaluation, and alleviation of potential risks that could jeopardize the success of change initiative implementation. Risks may entail employee resistance, goal misalignment, resource inadequacy, ineffective communication, or unintended repercussions that could impede the process. Effectively addressing these risks is crucial to facilitate a seamless transition and attain the desired outcomes.

The significance of risk management in organizational change lies in its proactive approach to tackling challenges and uncertainties that may surface throughout the change journey. By pinpointing potential risks early on, organizations can devise strategies to mitigate or eradicate these risks, thereby diminishing the likelihood of adverse repercussions. This proactive stance aids in establishing a more stable change environment, enabling organizations to anticipate and brace for potential hurdles rather than reacting to them post-occurrence.

Risk management is intricately linked to change readiness, denoting an organization's preparedness to execute and implement change successfully. It encompasses having the requisite resources, competencies, and support structures to navigate the change process effectively. Risk management bolsters change preparedness by identifying and remedying potential risks before they escalate into significant challenges. This state of readiness empowers organizations to adapt swiftly to changes, sustain momentum, and accomplish their objectives without major disruptions.

Moreover, risk management directly influences resistance to change, a prevalent risk in any change initiative. Resistance can emanate from diverse sources, such as apprehension of the unknown, loss of authority, perceived job security threats, or discomfort with novel procedures and technologies. By integrating risk management into the change process, organizations can unearth the underlying causes of resistance and formulate targeted strategies to address them. For instance, offering transparent communication regarding the rationale for change, providing training and assistance, and involving employees in decision-making can mitigate resistance and cultivate support for the change.

Furthermore, proficient risk management fosters trust and confidence among employees and stakeholders, which is pivotal for minimizing resistance. When employees witness the organization taking measures to anticipate and manage risks, they are more likely to feel reassured and bolstered during the change journey. This trust nurtures a positive outlook toward change and diminishes the likelihood of resistance.

In essence, risk management assumes a critical role in organizational change by identifying and mitigating potential risks, thereby enhancing change preparedness and diminishing resistance. Through proactive risk mitigation, organizations can foster a supportive change environment, heighten the prospects of successful outcomes, and ensure a seamless transition to novel operational paradigms. This approach curtails potential disruptions and cultivates a culture of resilience and adaptability, imperative for sustained success in an ever-evolving business landscape.

Another factor is the employee experience with past change initiatives. In our engagement with one organization, we encountered a familiar pattern. Two major organizational development initiatives, Total Quality Management (TQM) and Continuous Learning, had been launched enthusiastically within the past three years. Each lost momentum due to complacency and widespread burnout. By the time we were brought in, the workforce had grown skeptical, viewing the upcoming strategic planning process as just another "management pet project" unlikely to yield lasting change.

To address this climate of initiative fatigue and rebuild credibility, our approach focused on three core strategies. We openly acknowledged the past projects and validated the experiences of employees and managers. Rather than ignoring the unfulfilled promises of past efforts, we named them directly. This created space for honest dialogue and restored psychological safety, signaling that our approach would be to listen to their view at various stages of implementing this initiative, and address their needs as much as possible.

We also built upon what had been accomplished under the previous initiatives. For instance, we discussed how we use cause-and-effect diagrams along with the Mission-Drive Strategy Map to help identify and address systemic barriers to inclusion. We also discussed how developing inclusion competency requires continuous learning. This approach not only utilizes existing skills but also demonstrates that initiative we offered is a continuous improvement process akin to quality management.

Overall, an organization's readiness for change after an assessment report calls for a cultural shift is influenced by leadership commitment, awareness of the need for change, existing cultural adaptability, employee engagement, resource availability, change management competence, anticipation of resistance, measurement and feedback mechanisms, emotional readiness, and risk management. These factors collectively determine whether an organization is prepared to undertake the significant effort required to shift its culture and achieve its desired ECDI objectives.

Once the organization is prepared to design and develop a strategic plan, that is the next step.

Reducing Resistance to Change

Leading organizational change is like training for a marathon. Preparation involves dedication, setting a clear goal, and knowing that the path will be long and full of challenges. The ECDI leader helps the organization pace itself, ensuring it follows the action plan, providing support during difficult stretches, and celebrating the small victories along the way. Like a marathon, progress can be slow and steady, but with persistence and leadership, the finish line is always in sight. Change demands fostering and nurturing collaboration, effective communication, and a shared commitment to a successful journey. The leader helps the workforce imagine reaching a state in which the pain associated with not changing is replaced with the pleasure that comes with successful change.

The old saying, "You can lead a horse to water, but you can't make it drink," is no less true here. However, the ECDI practitioner's effectiveness depends on getting the horse to drink the water with minimum resistance. You cannot force the organization, but you can help mobilize it into action out of fear of the consequences of not changing, including making the change process as transparent and straightforward as possible.

Larry Greiner and Robert Metzger point out seven techniques to manage resistance (Greiner, L., & Metzger, R.,1983),

1. Co-opt the resistors by recruiting them on the steering committee or spending time with them informally to review the plans and findings.

2. Hold organization-wide information sessions to inform members of how changes affect them and solicit their feedback.

3. Uncover sacred cows within the organization and avoid attacking them.

4. Offer at least three strategies for implementing different change actions so members feel like they have choices. Solicit feedback on the options they favor, along with a ranking. Be open to hearing alternatives outside the list you have provided.

5. Propose experimentation to determine the best approach based on their limited use as a pilot.

6. Consider employing a novel or unconventional approach to address political views within the organization, particularly when other options risk deepening divisions among different groups. A creative solution can prevent perceptions of favoritism toward any particular

group. For example, some White Americans may feel threatened by mandatory racial equity initiatives. By framing equity as essential for the well-being of the entire organization and highlighting research showing when marginalized racial groups do not experience equity, no one enjoys it fully. This makes the message more relatable and inclusive for everyone.

7. Stress incentives to increase participation.

By following these strategies, organizations can effectively onboard their leadership to a ECDI initiative, creating a culture of equity and belonging.

The first key element to sustaining culture change is consistent and clear communication from leadership. Leaders must actively reinforce the reasons for the change, aligning it with the organization's vision and values. This means regularly communicating the benefits of the new culture, both through formal channels like meetings and email and informal channels such as casual conversations or storytelling. By making the case for the change visible and ongoing, leadership can ensure that employees understand its importance and relevance to their day-to-day work. Leaders should also model the desired behaviors to demonstrate their commitment and set an example for others.

Embedding the culture change into daily operations and processes is essential. This can be done by aligning the new values with business practices, including how decisions are made, how success is measured, and how employees are rewarded. For example, if collaboration and transparency are part of the new culture, systems, and tools that promote teamwork and openness should be implemented. Additionally, the performance management system should reflect the desired culture, incorporating metrics that measure business outcomes and behaviors that support the cultural shift. This alignment ensures that the organization's operations become part of the ECDI culture resulting from the change initiative.

Another critical factor is creating early wins and celebrating them. In the early stages of culture change, it's essential to highlight and reward successes that align with the new cultural direction. Increased sales to a population once difficult to reach, resulting from implementing new practices, can be exploited to celebrate the impact of the changes on the bottom line. Recognizing employees and teams who embody the new values reinforces the change and demonstrates that the organization values these behaviors. Celebrating small victories also builds confidence, showing that progress is being made and that the change is achievable. These early wins should be communicated widely across the organization to inspire others and build momentum.

Engagement and involvement from all employees is crucial for sustaining change. This means empowering employees at all levels to take ownership of the cultural shift by giving them opportunities to contribute ideas and feedback. Creating forums for discussion, such as focus groups, workshops, or town hall meetings, allows employees to voice their opinions and feel like active participants in the process. When employees feel a sense of ownership over the change, they are more likely to embrace it and help drive it forward. It's also important to address concerns and resistance openly, providing support and guidance to those struggling with the transition.

Providing ongoing training and development opportunities is another way to sustain culture change. Employees need the tools and skills to adapt to new ways of working, so offering workshops, coaching, or mentoring programs can help them adjust and grow. Continuous learning also keeps the momentum going by reinforcing the new behaviors and ensuring that employees have the resources they need to succeed in the changed environment. Consistency and resilience are vital. The organization must consistently reinforce the new culture through policies, actions, and leadership behavior. Any inconsistencies, such as leaders reverting to old habits or policies contradicting the desired values, can undermine the effort and cause confusion. All aspects of the organization, from hiring practices to promotions, should reflect the new culture to sustain the change.

Resilience is essential for sustaining organizational change because change involves uncertainty, resistance, and setbacks, which can lead to fatigue and frustration among employees. Resilient individuals and organizations are better equipped to adapt, recover, and stay engaged, even when slow progress or obstacles arise. When disruptions occur, whether due to internal factors like staffing changes or external pressures such as political or economic shifts, resilience helps maintain focus on long-term goals. It also builds trust and confidence, as employees are more likely to stay committed when they see leaders and coworkers responding constructively to challenges. In addition, resilience encourages a growth mindset. It allows organizations to view setbacks as opportunities to learn, improve, and refine their approach. This is especially important for cultural change initiatives, such as building an inclusive and equitable workplace, which require sustained effort over time.

Patience is related to resilience. As stated, organizational culture change is a gradual process that takes time to take root. Recognizing that setbacks may occur and being prepared to address them with a long-term perspective is essential. Patient leadership maintains a steady commitment to the change, even when slow progress or challenges arise. By staying the course and continuously reinforcing the new culture, the organization can gradually embed the change into its DNA and ensure its sustainability over time. Ultimately, resilience is the driving force that helps organizations navigate the complexities of change while maintaining momentum, engagement, and alignment with their vision.

Chapter 10 Implementation: Navigating the Transformative Journey

Creating an ECDI organizational culture is not a one-time event. It is a strategic and ongoing process that requires thoughtful planning, strong leadership, and sustained engagement at every level. A well-developed strategic plan serves as the foundation for this journey, but its success depends on how effectively it is communicated, implemented, and adapted over time. This phase of the ECDI initiative focuses on turning vision into action. From engaging stakeholders through transparent communication to aligning leadership, monitoring progress, and celebrating wins, each step plays a critical role in shifting organizational culture. What follows are key components and best practices to ensure that the strategic plan is not only understood and supported across the organization but also actively drives measurable and lasting change.

Communicate the Strategic Plan to All Stakeholders. Effective communication ensures that all stakeholders understand and support the strategic plan. Once the strategic plan is developed, communicate it widely across the organization to ensure everyone is aware of the goals, objectives, strategies, and actions. Use a variety of communication channels, such as internal newsletters, emails, meetings, and the organization's intranet, to share the plan and provide regular updates on progress. Tailor the communication to different audiences to ensure it resonates and is relevant to their roles and responsibilities. Encouraging open dialogue and feedback about the strategic plan helps build buy-in and commitment from employees at all levels and fosters a culture of inclusion and continuous improvement.

Implement the Strategic Plan and Monitor Progress. With the strategic plan completed, the strategies and tactics are implemented according to the established timeline. Monitor progress regularly to ensure that actions are carried out as planned and objectives are met. Regular monitoring involves reviewing progress reports, analyzing metrics and KPIs, and conducting check-ins with those responsible for leading various aspects of the initiative. This helps identify any challenges or barriers early on and allows for timely adjustments to the plan as needed. As mentioned, it is also important to celebrate successes and recognize achievements along the way to maintain momentum and motivation. Acknowledging progress reinforces the organization's commitment to diversity, equity, and inclusion and encourages continued efforts.

Evaluate and Adjust the Strategic Plan as Needed. Continuous evaluation is essential to ensure the strategic plan remains effective and aligned with the organization's evolving needs and goals. Regularly evaluate the success of the ECDI initiative by analyzing metrics and KPIs, gathering feedback from stakeholders, and assessing the overall impact on the organization. Any adjustments based on the evaluation are communicated as needed to inform the workforce of challenges or gaps to be addressed for improvement. By following these steps, organizations can continue to provide a clear roadmap for achieving culture change goals and fostering engagement and commitment.

Ensure that Culture Change Is Led through Top and Middle Management. Management is seldom a monolithic group. Some managers and leaders will react favorably toward the initiative, while others may be waiting gleefully for the efforts to fail. The majority probably will be complacent as other matters more important to them capture their attention. Get to know as many of these movers and shakers as possible. The more the ECDI practitioner and their team are viewed as working on behalf of the organization, the more trust in the initiative will grow.

It is important to choose the right approach, prioritize employee engagement, and align culture change with the company's overall strategy and priorities to ensure that organizational culture change direction is led through top management.

Implementing an ECDI initiative requires a dedicated team with the necessary skills and resources to execute the strategy. The team is responsible for:

- Utilizing a project management system. Project management is the key to organizational change. A system that incorporates the strategic initiative action items and performs tracking will help keep the pulse of progress and provide feedback to the leadership team on a regular basis.
- Developing and implementing a communication plan. Communicating the ECDI initiative to the leadership, middle management, and all employees is critical for onboarding them.
- Providing training and development opportunities.
- Addressing any issues that arise during implementation.

Embarking on a change initiative to create an inclusive, equitable, and culturally diverse organizational culture is a transformative journey. It requires patience, persistence, and a willingness to learn and adapt along the way.

Here are some insights to help navigate this transformative journey:

- Monitor Progress and Evaluate Outcomes: Regularly monitor the progress of the change initiatives and evaluate the outcomes. This will help identify areas of success and areas that require further attention. Use data and metrics to measure the impact of the change initiatives and make necessary adjustments as needed.
- Celebrate Successes: Recognize and celebrate the successes achieved along the way. This will help build momentum, boost morale, and reinforce the importance of the change initiatives. Celebrate both small and big wins to keep employees motivated and engaged.
- Address Challenges and Resistance: Anticipate and address challenges and resistance that may arise during the change process. Be open to feedback and address concerns promptly. Provide support and resources to help employees overcome barriers and adapt to the changes.

Implementing a diversity and inclusion initiative requires a skilled team to manage data collection, track progress, and use project management systems for monitoring and feedback.

Key tasks include creating a communication plan to engage leadership and employees, offering training, and addressing challenges. Success depends on regularly evaluating outcomes, adjusting strategies, celebrating achievements to maintain momentum, and managing resistance with openness and support. This transformative journey toward inclusion demands patience, adaptability, and ongoing engagement to foster an equitable and culturally diverse organizational culture.

Monitor and Evaluate Progress

Monitoring and evaluating progress is critical to ensure the success of the strategies and tactics. Develop a robust continuous evaluation approach, including qualitative and quantitative measures, such as participation rates in training programs, changes in employee survey scores, and feedback from ERGs. Use the data to adjust strategies and tactics, ensuring continuous improvement and alignment with the organization's ECDI vision. If successfully recruiting employees for training is hampered by competing training priorities or management's concerns about training fatigue, creative strategies will be needed to keep the initiative moving forward.

One way we increase client support is to offer a few sessions to managers before the larger workforce is recruited. We provide managers with training tailored to their specific needs, which enables them to see the value to the organization as a whole. Of course, this requires expert training design, development, and delivery skills. Learning about their needs during the assessment phase for strategic planning provides insights into their pain spots and training content to address them. One experience involved providing mandatory management racial equity training to a group of managers. One of the participants happened to have considerable influence in the organization. They championed our training afterward and made it possible for our training to be included in the annual compliance training sessions for all employees. We no longer had to recruit participants, and the agency's training services set up the training room and our slide deck for each session.

Following a structured approach, we were able to position our project for success better. Continuous assessment enables the ECDI team to be agile in managing risk by keeping a pulse on the organization's current state.

Reassessment

Reassessment is the process of revisiting an organization's ECDI landscape after implementing culture change initiatives. It involves evaluating whether the recommended strategies and actions taken since the initial assessment have effectively addressed identified gaps, barriers, or opportunities and whether measurable progress has been achieved in building equity and inclusion competency. Of course, the best indicator is a shift towards higher equity and inclusion competency stages.

The key components include data collection, outcome evaluation, updated equity and inclusion competency assessments, and strategy adjustment if warranted by the data. Data collection requires gathering updated qualitative and quantitative data through surveys, interviews, focus groups, and policy reviews to compare against baseline findings from the initial assessment. Measure the effectiveness of implemented initiatives by analyzing metrics such as workforce diversity, employee engagement, retention rates, inclusion indices, and overall organizational climate. Assessing changes in organizational competencies related to equity, cultural diversity, and inclusion to determine barriers that were removed and any remaining barriers, increases in inclusion and equity competency, and elimination of identified persistent equity challenges.

Engaging employees and other stakeholders in the process helps ensure their voices and experiences are heard while building transparency and trust. This leads to better insights into how the changes affect the workforce. When data shows a need for adjustments, the strategy is updated to improve underperforming initiatives or address new challenges. Regularly reassessing progress keeps organizations moving forward, recognizing achievements, tackling obstacles, and creating lasting, meaningful change.

Chapter 11: Mastering Inclusion Competency in the Workplace

Inclusion competency is essential for creating an ECDI culture because it equips leaders and employees with the knowledge, awareness, skills, and tools to promote equity and inclusion actively. It goes beyond well-meaning intentions by enabling individuals to recognize and address inequities in support of collaborating across all workforce levels. In doing so, it helps reduce the effects of organizational stratification. Without this competency, efforts to build an equitable and diverse culture will fall short, as policies and intentions alone cannot transform a well-established culture, deeply ingrained mindsets, and behaviors that maintain the status quo. Leaders and employees with inclusion competency are better prepared to notice even subtle inequities, interrupt exclusionary practices, and advocate for meaningful change. This creates inclusive interactions and decisions, trust, and a shared sense of valuing differences, which are the cornerstones of a thriving ECDI culture.

In an equity-centered organization, individuals at all levels volunteer to adopt Inclusion Competency skills to improve how they interact, lead, and collaborate. These skills go beyond basic cultural diversity awareness, enabling people to work effectively across differences, challenge systemic barriers, and foster inclusive, high-trust environments. At the individual level, employees are expected to cultivate self-awareness of cultural values and beliefs, knowledge about what equity means and how inequities undermine individual and team performance, and the skills needed to effectively navigate cultural differences, identify inequities, and foster equity. They value allyship and learning how to support colleagues from marginalized backgrounds.

Teams within equity-centered organizations establish shared norms that prioritize respectful dialogue, inclusion, and psychological safety. This involves using collaborative practices that bring inequities to the surface and foster joint problem-solving. Team members are encouraged to take shared responsibility for ensuring equitable participation, fair voice, and collective accountability for inclusion.

Supervisors play a critical role in creating inclusive team dynamics. They are responsible for identifying and mitigating bias in performance evaluations, coaching styles, and disciplinary actions. Inclusive competency supervision is valued which compels them to learn how to adapt to the diverse cultural and developmental needs of employees, particularly those who have historically been excluded. Managers are equipped to identify structural barriers by using disaggregated data and employee feedback. Their work involves cultivating inclusive team cultures that normalize equity practices and challenge exclusionary norms. Equitable and inclusive talent management is valued as a key competency to ensure fair access to professional development, advancement opportunities, and aligning recognition and evaluation systems with organizational equity goals.

Executives and senior leaders are responsible for stewarding systemic equity literacy. They value equity and must understand how historical inequities and organizational stratification influence access, outcomes, and workplace climate. Leaders are expected to embed equity into strategy, budgeting, and performance management systems. They also play a vital role in modeling allyship across hierarchical levels by forming authentic partnerships with underrepresented staff and sponsoring bottom-up leadership and innovation. These competencies are not isolated to specific roles. They form a cohesive organizational fabric where equity is not merely aspirational but operationalized across daily practice.

In short, inclusion competency turns values into action. It ensures that cultural diversity is not just present but fully leveraged and equity is not just a goal but an everyday practice. This section explores some talent management "best practices" for developing Inclusion Competency across key areas for organizational success, such as recruitment, legal compliance, and allyship. It is mostly musing based on what works for our clients. The goal is to get your creative juices flowing.

Table 2: Inclusion Competency Components by Organizational Level

ORGANIZATIONAL LEVEL	KEY COMPONENTS FOCUS
Individual Contributors	Self-awareness, equity communication, allyship
Teams	Equity norms, inclusive collaboration, shared ownership
Supervisors	Bias reduction, coaching for inclusion, participatory leadership
Managers	Structural awareness, inclusive culture building, equitable talent management
Executives	Strategic equity vision, systemic change leadership, top-down and cross-level allyship

Strengthening the Workforce Through Inclusive and Equitable Hiring Practices

Recruitment is often the first gateway to workplace cultural diversity, yet without intentional strategies, organizations risk perpetuating systemic barriers that exclude historically marginalized and excluded group talent. Inclusive and equitable hiring practices ensure that organizations attract, recruit, and retain diverse talent, creating a workforce that reflects a broad range of experiences, perspectives, and skills. By actively removing barriers to hiring fairness, such as biased job descriptions, limited outreach, and restrictive hiring criteria, companies can tap into a wider talent pool, increasing their ability to identify and hire the best and brightest among a culturally diverse talent pool. Structured hiring processes, standardized interview questions, and diverse hiring panels help mitigate unconscious bias, ensuring candidates are evaluated based on their skills and potential rather than subjective preferences.

Bias in hiring and promotions can hinder an organization's ability to acquire and leverage its talent fully. Bias mitigation strategies, such as blind resume screening, structured evaluations, and implicit bias training, reduce the impact of practices that disadvantage qualified historically marginalized and excluded group candidates. When organizations implement these strategies, they foster a culture of fairness, where hiring and advancement decisions are based on merit and competence rather than unreliable personal preferences. This approach leads to a more dynamic and capable workforce, where talent is recognized and nurtured regardless of background.

Equitable Career Pathways: Building Long-Term Success for All Employees

Beyond hiring, organizations must ensure that employees have equal access to professional development and leadership opportunities. Equitable career pathways—such as mentorship programs, sponsorship initiatives, and skills-based promotions—help bridge gaps in advancement that often disproportionately affect historically marginalized and excluded group employees. Transparent performance evaluations, professional development programs, and leadership pipelines for underrepresented talent create a workplace where employees feel valued and invested in their long-term success.

Driving Innovation and Engagement

A workforce built on inclusive and equitable hiring practices thrives on diversity of thought, leading to increased creativity, problem-solving, and innovation. Research shows that culturally diverse teams make better decisions and are more effective at addressing complex challenges. Furthermore, when employees see that their organization prioritizes fairness and inclusion, they are more engaged, motivated, and committed to the company's success. An inclusive culture fosters collaboration, psychological safety, and trust, which are key drivers of high-performance teams. By embedding equity into every stage of the employee lifecycle, from hiring to career advancement, organizations strengthen their workforce, enhance innovation, and create a thriving, engaged workplace where all employees can succeed.

Best Practices for Mitigating Legal Risk

Legal compliance is equally essential in fostering an equitable workplace. With shifting regulations and increasing scrutiny on DEI initiatives, organizations must navigate complex legal landscapes to ensure that policies and practices align with anti-discrimination laws while upholding their cultural diversity commitments. This section will highlight legal considerations, risk management strategies, and lessons from recent case studies to help organizations stay compliant and proactive.

Implementing the ECDI approach in talent management is a powerful strategy for fostering workplace diversity and fairness. However, organizations must proactively address legal risks to ensure compliance with anti-discrimination laws while advancing their ECDI goals to prevent major setbacks. Organizations must ensure that all ECDI-related policies align with federal, state, and local employment laws to prevent legal challenges. Title VII of the Civil Rights Act (1964), for example, prohibits employment discrimination based on race, color, religion, sex, or national origin. The Americans with Disabilities Act (ADA) requires reasonable accommodations and prohibits disability-based discrimination. The Age Discrimination in Employment Act (ADEA) protects employees aged 40 and older from age-based discrimination, while the Equal Pay Act (EPA) mandates equal pay for equal work regardless of gender. Regular legal audits and policy reviews should be conducted to ensure that DEI initiatives comply with these regulations.

Organizations must establish clearly defined equity principles that guide daily operations and minimize the risk of reverse discrimination or unfair treatment claims. In light of recent legal decisions against affirmative action, it is imperative to avoid using quotas. While setting numerical goals for recruiting historically marginalized and excluded groups, such as women, into leadership roles has historically improved access and mobility for them, such practices are no longer legally sanctioned.

The Fourteenth Amendment was adopted initially after the Civil War to protect formerly enslaved Black people from discrimination and oppression. It resulted in an equity approach to creating fairness It was later interpreted to apply equally to all Americans. This shift from an equity to an equality approach came at the expense of targeted efforts to address the unique needs of Black Americans. Today, the amendment is frequently used to challenge rather than support initiatives to address the lingering effects of systemic inequities.

Balancing ECDI initiatives with legal protections requires proper training for decision-makers. Leaders need training to recognize practices that inadvertently result in disparities, avoid using quotas, and identify disparate treatment. Equitable accommodation practices must also be implemented to support diverse employees without creating legal risks. No matter how inequitable an organization has been, no one is left behind in the ECDI approach, even those responsible for orchestrating inequities. Mandatory DEI and legal compliance training ensures that leaders and management understand both the ethical and legal aspects of talent management.

A strong documentation strategy is key to defending against potential legal claims. Organizations must maintain detailed records of hiring and promotion decisions, including justifications. Tracking workforce demographic trends helps assess progress and identify potential risk areas while conducting regular pay equity analyses ensures that disparities are identified and corrected.

Training content needs to be documented and analyzed for equity and using. A training content equity checklist tool is ideal for the records. To avoid legal challenges, especially in response to recent litigation against DEI programs, companies should ensure that ECDI initiatives remain voluntary and non-coercive. Diversity training should be encouraged rather than mandated, emphasizing inclusive leadership and workplace culture rather than identity-based preferences. When mandatory training is necessary, it needs to include different perspectives. During a contract to deliver mandatory racial equity training to a very large public sector organization, the client requested a meeting as the federal government's demands for removing DEI in organizations rose. We assured them that our training does not contribute to legal risk. Our training content and exceptionally high course evaluations supported our claims.

Affinity groups, mentorship programs, and sponsorship initiatives should be open to all employees, regardless of background. Avoiding exclusionary or preferential practices helps maintain legal defensibility while advancing DEI goals. Since legal and social landscapes constantly evolve, organizations must stay proactive in compliance efforts. Conducting annual ECDI mini audits and running the results by legal counsel helps assess risks. Regularly incorporating employee feedback mechanisms further ensures that initiatives remain inclusive and non-discriminatory. By documenting ECDI implementation, organizations can demonstrate a commitment to compliance and fairness, reducing legal vulnerabilities.

Inclusion-Equity Competency Training

Equity-centered training provides a learning environment where participants examine their shared mission, the role of equity in achieving it, and its influence on workplace culture and productivity. It deepens their understanding of the challenges that arise from unmanaged cultural diversity in hierarchical organizations.

Participants explore how the workplace mirrors society's socioeconomic distribution, in which historically excluded groups, particularly BIPOC individuals and women, are concentrated in lower levels of the organization, and the historically majority and included group at the top. This awareness provides participants with an understanding of how workplace inequities reflect broader systemic injustices that erode fairness and hinder teamwork. By connecting these disparities to historical barriers in both society and the workplace, the training fosters a deeper commitment to driving meaningful equity reduction culture change

A transit agency engaged Diversity Training University International's consulting team to design racial equity training for executives, managers, and line workers. We developed tailored programs: one for executives and upper management, another for lower-level managers and supervisors, and a third for line workers. Each training covered the history of societal inequities from the Civil War to anti-Asian laws and the civil rights movement, linking past legalized discrimination to persistent workplace disparities. Participants explored how different racial and cultural groups have faced and responded to inequity, shifting from mutual support to competitive relations. Managers and supervisors learn tools to identify, manage, and reduce workplace inequities, while line workers gain strategies to recognize and address inequitable or uncivil treatment among colleagues.

One of the lessons used in the racial equity training asks the participants to identify their common mission in their workplace. Far too many say their paycheck or getting home to their families safely.

Others say service to the. Then I tell them, "Let me know if I'm wrong, but what you all have in common is supporting the transportation services needed to get people from one location to another safely, effectively, and efficiently." Everyone agrees. The lesson learned is that it is easy to lose the shared mission and keeping it in the forefront is necessary to understand how policies, practices, and interactions that undermine the mission need to be addressed.

We also show an image of how the societal hierarchy is segmented (i.e., people grouped on the top, middle, and bottom of the socioeconomic strata) and predicted by race and gender. A similar hierarchy is shown with the labels changed from socioeconomic status differences to segmentation based on race and gender. Darker colored figures are over-represented at the bottom, and the top is filled with white colored figures. During the training with the transit "bus" drivers, we display a triangulation for the color-coded workplace hierarchy. At the same time, asking participants who has the most thankless and dangerous job in the agency. Those stereotypes as belonging to the lower-tier groups are always expectedly to say, "We do." Then I tell them to look around the room. What they see are mostly Asian, Black, and Latino/Hispanic bodies and mostly males.

The next thing I ask them during the exercise is what the percentage of White Americans in their organization is. We discuss how it is a relatively low percentage before I ask what that group's percentage is in the executive team. They struggle with the correct answer. When I inform them that it is about fifteen percent of the workforce and that historically majority and included groups make up 90-95% of the executives, they are surprised. Whether in upper management or entry-level roles, participants engage with history lessons that reveal how inequities arise, their lasting effects, and how these dynamics show up in the workplace. The training helps them recognize how they may unintentionally contribute to inequity through microinequities often stemming from a lack of shared purpose and collaboration.

This summary highlights how conversations about race and inequity can take place without blame, shame, or complaint. The result is a mandatory training that is widely appreciated, as participants feel included rather than singled out. In turn, the organization strengthens its equity competency in alignment with its racial equity goals.

Allyship

Allyship is the active, consistent, and intentional effort to advocate for marginalized individuals or groups to achieve equity, inclusion, and cultural diversity. True allyship requires action, self-awareness, continuous education, and accountability. It goes beyond passive agreement with DEI practices. Key aspects of allyship include:

1. Recognizing Privilege & Power Dynamics. Allies acknowledge systemic inequities and their implications. They understand how power and privilege maintain inequities and use their position to challenge unfair structures and lack of Inclusion Competency without blaming, shaming, or complaining. This includes learning about and understanding how race, gender, class, and other identities shape workplace experiences.

2. Listening and Learning. Effective allies seek to understand historically marginalized and excluded groups' experiences, concerns, and perspectives. This involves active listening, educating oneself about bias, and being open to feedback and personal growth. They do more listening than talking and learn how to support historically marginalized and excluded groups effectively.

3. Taking Action & Advocacy. Allyship is not performative. It requires real action to challenge discrimination, support equitable policies, and create inclusive environments. Actions can include mentoring underrepresented employees, advocating for fair hiring and promotion practices, or calling out bias and microaggressions in the workplace.

4. <u>Sharing Power & Creating Opportunities.</u> True allies use their influence and networks to create opportunities for marginalized individuals. This can mean sponsoring BIPOC employees for leadership roles, ensuring diverse voices are heard in decision-making, and pushing for equity in pay and career advancement.

5. <u>Holding Oneself & Others Accountable.</u> Allyship requires ongoing reflection and accountability. Not just words but consistent, meaningful engagement. Allies should be open to being corrected, acknowledge mistakes, and commit to continuous learning and advocacy.

Allyship in the Workplace

In an organizational setting, allyship plays a crucial role in talent management by enhancing communication, engagement, and equity. When leaders and employees actively support historically marginalized and excluded group colleagues, they disrupt exclusionary patterns and cultivate a culture where everyone experiences fairness. As mentioned earlier, organizations are typically structured hierarchically. With increasing cultural diversity in a hierarchical organization, women and historically marginalized and excluded groups tend to be unfairly overrepresented at the lower ranks. In contrast, historically majority and included groups are overrepresented among executives if there is no plan for managing cultural differences. Executives occupy the top tier, followed by managers and supervisors in the middle, while line workers, who disproportionately tend to be BIPOC and women, fill the lower segments of the hierarchy. This structure frequently results in a lack of communication, poor collegiality, and disengagement across levels, reinforcing exclusionary practices that hinder genuine workplace equity. Only intentional cultural diversity management can protect against entrenched racial and gender inequities.

While many DEI efforts focus on policies and training, allyship is a powerful yet often overlooked practice for fostering inclusion and equity within hierarchical organizations. When executives, managers, and supervisors act as allies, they can bridge the gaps among organizational tiers, improve communication, and create a culture of support and shared responsibility. Designing and implementing an intentional allyship plan is a critical step toward ensuring that historically marginalized and excluded group employees feel heard, valued, empowered, and treated fairly in the workplace, which increases their engagement.

The Role of Allyship Across Organizational Levels

Systemic change starts at the top. Executives set the strategic direction, allocate resources, and shape the organizational culture. Making their commitment to equity not only influential but essential. Yet, despite their power, executives often remain disconnected from the day-to-day realities of frontline staff. This disconnect undermines efforts to build an inclusive workplace and can result in well-meaning initiatives falling short of their goals.

To create meaningful and lasting change, executive leaders must move beyond statements of support and engage directly with those most impacted by inequities in the workplace. This means modeling allyship through action, fostering authentic relationships across the organizational hierarchy, and embedding equity into decision-making processes. When executives demonstrate that inclusion is not a peripheral initiative but a core leadership responsibility, they set a tone that resonates throughout the organization.

Executives: Setting the Tone for Systemic Change. Executives have the greatest influence over an organization's culture and policies, yet they are often the most disconnected from frontline employees. This disconnect creates a lack of accountability for equity efforts and prevents leadership from understanding the lived experiences of those at the bottom of the hierarchy.

An effective allyship plan at the executive level should include partnering with one or two managers and one or two supervisors to:

- Offer regular, structured engagement with line workers through forums, roundtables, and listening sessions to understand workplace challenges from their perspective.
- Create formal and informal employee leadership development programs, ensuring that promotion pipelines are clear and equitable.
- Identify equity barriers and consider ways to align policy with equity goals, ensuring that strategic decisions consider the impact on lower-level employees.

Executives must actively participate in cross-level dialogues and publicly committing to equity-driven organizational change. Demonstrating allyship validates the experiences of marginalized employees and sends a message that inclusion is a leadership priority, not just an HR function.

Managers and Supervisors: Building Bridges and Fostering Collegiality. Managers and supervisors comprise the middle segment of the organizational hierarchy. These employees play a crucial role in shaping the daily work environment. However, due to the pressure to meet operational goals, they often default to transactional leadership practices, which include enforcing rules and policies at the cost of inclusion and team cohesion. The result is a lack of trust, poor collegiality, and disengagement, particularly for BIPOC employees who experience limited access to mentorship, support, and professional growth opportunities.

An effective allyship plan for managers and supervisors should include:

- Structured mentorship and advocacy for employees in the lower hierarchy to provide career guidance and professional development opportunities.

- Training on inclusive leadership equips managers with skills to support and uplift BIPOC employees rather than merely supervising their tasks.
- Accountability measures ensure that middle-tier leaders' evaluations include their ability to foster inclusion and communication across levels.

When supervisors and managers serve as advocates for frontline workers, they help break down silos, reduce power imbalances, and create an environment of mutual respect and collaboration.

Frontline Workers: Recognizing and Leveraging Allyship. For BIPOC employees and women in lower segments of the organization, allyship provides an opportunity to gain visibility, access, and support that they are often denied in traditional workplace structures. However, allyship must be intentional and reciprocal, which means that frontline workers also need mechanisms to hold allies accountable for their commitments. An effective allyship plan for line workers should include (1) formal channels for feedback, ensuring that employees can voice concerns and suggest improvements without fear of retaliation, (2) opportunities for direct engagement with leadership, allowing BIPOC employees to share experiences, challenges, and aspirations with decision-makers, and (3) recognition of allyship efforts, ensuring that executives, managers, and supervisors are acknowledged and held accountable for their commitments to equity.

When lower-tier employees see and experience genuine allyship, their sense of belonging, job satisfaction, and engagement improve, reducing the barriers to upward mobility that have historically limited their growth.

Implementing an Effective Allyship Plan

For an allyship strategy to be successful, it must be institutionalized rather than treated as an informal or symbolic gesture. Organizations can implement a formal allyship initiative that includes:

- Allyship Training for Executives, Managers, and Supervisors. Educating leadership on the impact of workplace inequities and how to support marginalized employees actively.
- Cross-Level Partnership Programs. Pairing executives with frontline workers and managers builds meaningful relationships that reduce power imbalances and foster communication.
- Equity Accountability Metrics. Tracking mentorship participation, promotion rates, retention data, and employee feedback offer data needed to assess the effectiveness of allyship efforts.
- Transparent Communication Channels. Creating safe spaces for employees to discuss workplace challenges ensures that their concerns reach decision-makers without fear of retaliation.

Summary

A hierarchical workplace does not have to be a barrier to equity. An allyship program that reaches all organizational levels plays an important role in reducing disparities, improving communication, and fostering a culture of collegiality and mutual support. By designing and implementing an intentional allyship plan, organizations can dismantle exclusionary practices, empower BIPOC employees, and ensure that DEI efforts lead to real, structural change. When executives, managers, and supervisors actively engage as allies, they disrupt traditional power structures and create an environment where everyone, regardless of rank or background, can thrive.

Building an inclusive and equitable workplace requires more than good intentions; it demands strategic action, informed decision-making, and continuous learning. This section explored key ECDI best practices in recruitment, legal compliance, and allyship, offering practical insights drawn from real-world applications rather than purely theory. Inclusive and equitable hiring practices expand access to culturally diverse talent by removing systemic barriers and mitigating bias in selection processes. Equitable career pathways ensure all employees have opportunities for advancement, fostering engagement and long-term success. A diverse workforce drives innovation by leveraging different perspectives and creating a culture of fairness, trust, and collaboration.

Legal compliance remains a critical component of equity efforts. Organizations must align policies with anti-discrimination laws, avoid quotas, and ensure that DEI initiatives remain voluntary and non-coercive. Documentation, legal audits, and leadership training help mitigate risks while maintaining a commitment to fairness.

Equity-centered training deepens participants' understanding of historical inequities and their modern workplace impact. By focusing on shared organizational missions rather than blame, these programs encourage open discussions and collective problem-solving. Real-world examples from transit agency training illustrate how engaging, fact-based approaches foster awareness and action.

Allyship fosters equity through communication and support at all organizational levels. Executives interact with frontline employees, build leadership pipelines, and align policies with equity objectives. The managers and supervisors mentor BIPOC employees, encourage inclusive leadership, and ensure accountability. Line workers receive structured feedback channels, leadership involvement, and recognition of allyship contributions. Institutionalizing allyship via an initiative that involves training, partnerships, and accountability measures supports enduring workplace equity and inclusion. By integrating these best practices, organizations can move beyond performative DEI efforts and cultivate a workplace where inclusion and equity are embedded in every aspect of operations, decision-making, and daily interactions.

Conclusion

In concluding "Reimagining Fairness: An Equity, Cultural Diversity, Inclusion Competency Approach," it is essential to underscore the significance of adopting a creative coexistence perspective when designing, developing, and implementing measures to create inclusive and equitable organizations. Historically, DEI initiatives have too often concentrated on efforts to include and develop those in the lower ranks of the organizational hierarchy, inadvertently prioritizing equality practices that, while well-intentioned and vital, have placed organizations in legal jeopardy. When poorly conceived practices result in historically majority Americans feeling discriminated against, they understandably mobilize their grievances. This approach offered in this book harmonizes the workforce's needs to be treated fairly and as partners in meeting the strategic goals, which include managing business risk management and sustaining the initiative.

The path forward requires a balanced approach that integrates the aspirations of the workforce with the financial and risk management priorities of organizations. By embedding equity and inclusion competency principles into the core business strategy, organizations can create environments where equity and inclusion are not just serving social justice ideals but operational realities. We have witnessed the benefits indirectly with each shareholder's support for DEI in response to conservative organizations' attacks. Less than two percent are willing to vote against their self-interest. A balanced approach ensures that DEI initiatives are not only ethically sound but also legally robust and strategically aligned with business goals.

As organizations navigate the complexities of a diverse and dynamic workforce, embracing a creative coexistence model will be crucial. Equity, cultural diversity, and inclusion competency initiatives foster a culture where all employees feel valued and empowered, while also safeguarding the organization's legal and financial interests. By doing so, organizations can achieve sustainable success, driving innovation and resilience in an ever-evolving global marketplace. The journey toward true inclusion and equity is ongoing, and it is through strategic alignment and creative coexistence that organizations will thrive in the future.

It should be clear that the journey toward creating an equitable, culturally diverse, and inclusive workplace is challenging, rewarding, and possible. This book provides a comprehensive roadmap for organizations committed to transforming their cultures and embracing cultural diversity and equity as core values. By understanding the complexities of work and implementing data-driven continuous improvement plans that align with organizational values, leaders can foster environments where everyone feels valued and empowered. The insights and strategies outlined in this book emphasize the importance of continuous learning, adaptation, and commitment to change. Organizations must regularly assess their progress, engage stakeholders, and refine their approaches to ensure that equity and inclusion competency initiatives are not just temporary projects but integral components of their identity and operations.

Ultimately, the success of these efforts lies in the ability to create a culture where inclusion and equity are not merely goals but fundamental values that drive innovation, collaboration, and success. By embracing this vision, organizations can unlock the full potential of the modern workforce, leading to enhanced performance, greater employee satisfaction, and a more potent competitive edge in the global marketplace.

As the work continues, let this book serve as a guide and inspiration for leaders and practitioners dedicated to making meaningful and lasting change. Together, we can build a future where cultural diversity is not only celebrated but also recognized as a vital asset that enriches our organizations and society as a whole.

Epilogue: Cultural Diversity Always Wins

The idea that cultural diversity always prevails is backed by a strong mix of evidence, evolving legal decisions, organizational practices, and social advocacy. These efforts show that promoting cultural diversity has transitioned from being a moral, legal, or social imperative to a strategic advantage that fosters innovation, profitability, and resilience. The talent management shift and bottom-line DEI implementation results have successfully established DEI as a cornerstone of modern success and progress.

The demographic shift is a reality and ongoing. The efforts of those threatened by the wide acceptance of DEI to do away with the talent management solution offer evidence of its effectiveness. Well-intentioned but poorly trained DEI practitioners have implemented some misguided practices that are, at best, exclusive of the historical majority team members and, at worst, legally unsound. Their approaches are also oppositional to established meritocracy values, even if poorly conceived. Misguided diversity best practices have far too often been implemented under the assumption that "if everyone else is doing it and getting away with it, then we should, too." Human resource management has endured similar challenges. The same is true for equity and inclusion.

Many believed DEI initiatives were not scientifically sound enough to make a difference in organizations. Today, however, they are widely recognized as essential to modern institutions. In fact, organizations that have surveyed their stakeholders report less than two percent opposition to continuing DEI efforts. The success of companies like Apple, Goldman Sachs, Costco, Salesforce, and Patagonia is helping to shift public perception, while the increasing presence of culturally diverse, DEI-committed generations in the workforce underscores the long-term relevance and necessity of these initiatives.

The bumpy road to becoming an established institutional resource requires remaining committed, continuing to benefit from implementation, evidence-based practices, and getting beyond counting heads and celebrating cultural holidays. Cultural diversity will win even more once more organizations embed it into daily operations in ways that challenge the outdated and exclusive policies and practices that make it difficult to enjoy the full benefits and potential. Addressing the assumption that the workforce and business leaders have competing interests is an important part of the endeavor.

Costco's stockholders did not vote to sustain the DEI efforts from a moral or social justice perspective. They did so because they understood that it contributed to the company's success—their bottom line. A DEI commitment and programs do not guarantee legal protection for Costco. That depends on auditing existing programs for legal soundness as well as how potential legal problems are addressed based on the results. The city of Seattle and Thomas Jefferson School of Science and Technology prevailed in defending their initiatives because they emphasized equity without the use of quotas or excluding historically majority and included groups. Their open secret is to focus on those in the bottom segments who struggle to gain access to opportunities and resources many take for granted, such as a supermarket in close distance and accessible, cost-effective public transportation.

The journey toward an ECDI culture is not a one-time initiative but an ongoing commitment to transforming organizational culture. As explored throughout this book, true DEI integration requires more than policies and compliance. It demands a strategic, systemic shift in how organizations approach equity and inclusion.

The book examined the complex legal, procedural, and strategic cultural landscapes that shape DEI efforts, the limitations of traditional best practices, and the structural barriers that stubbornly resist cultural change. Through the ECDI Organizational Culture Change Approach, we have outlined a path for organizations to move beyond surface-level diversity initiatives and embed equity and inclusion into their core operations.

The ECDI approach provides organizations with a roadmap to:
- Assess the current culture and its structural barriers.
- Develop a strategic plan for cultural transformation.
- Implement sustainable, systemic changes that prioritize equity.
- Navigate legal and political challenges while maintaining progress.
- Sustain long-term DEI impact by fostering equity and inclusion competency.

DEI is at a crossroads. Some organizations will rise to the challenge, leading toward equitable and inclusive workplaces. Others may become paralyzed by legal risk aversion. One thing is clear: Organizations must commit to removing barriers to fairness, cultivating cultural transformation, and developing inclusion competency to move beyond aspirations to enduring realities. As organizations continue to evolve, the future of DEI will depend on leaders who are willing to challenge outdated assumptions, rethink traditional approaches, and embed equity into talent management and decision-making processes. The road ahead may be complex, but the stakes are too high to retreat. Organizations that embrace ECDI as a strategic imperative will not only create more inclusive workplaces but will also drive innovation, performance, and social progress

As I conclude this book, I encourage you to reflect on how you can apply these insights within your own organization. The journey toward cultural diversity, equity, and inclusion is ongoing, requiring dedication, perseverance, and a willingness to learn and grow. The future of DEI is in our hands, and the work we do today will shape the workplaces and societies of tomorrow. By embracing the principles outlined in this book, organizations can create a sustainable path to a more inclusive and equitable future where all individuals have the opportunity to thrive, and the competition will struggle to keep up. The work continues.

Glossary of Terms

Assessment Report

A document summarizing key insights, findings, and recommendations from an assessment, used to guide decision-making and action planning in an organization.

BIPOC

An acronym for Black, Indigenous, and People of Color, used to highlight the unique experiences and challenges faced by these groups.

Continuous Improvement Plan

Continuous Improvement Planning is an intentional, ongoing process in which leaders and teams regularly assess organizational practices, identify areas for enhancement, set measurable goals, and implement incremental changes to drive progress towards strategic goals over time. It empowers leaders to foster a culture of reflection, accountability, and adaptability, ensuring the organization continually evolves to meet emerging challenges and opportunities.

Unlike a strategic plan, which establishes long-term vision, priorities, and broad organizational goals over a defined period (typically 3–5 years), continuous improvement planning focuses on real-time, iterative adjustments to operations and practices. While the strategic plan sets the direction, continuous improvement ensures that progress toward those goals remains responsive, measurable, and aligned with day-to-day realities. Together, they provide complementary leadership tools—one for setting the course, the other for staying agile and effective along the way.

Cultural Diversity

Cultural diversity is defined as the norms, laws, and taboos that shape and govern a shared cultural identity among a group of people.

While the term was common in social science literature, corporate America embraced "diversity" as both a business imperative and a moral obligation as a result of the work of Roosevelt Thomas, who coined the term managing diversity. The term "cultural diversity in the workplace" gained traction in human resources, organizational development, and management fields during the 1990s. Today, the cultural aspect has been dropped to expand DEI efforts to be inclusive of groups with members who do not have a unique set of cultural practices, such as military and neurodivergent employees under diversity of thought.

DEI

Diversity, Equity, and Inclusion (DEI) is a framework for promoting fair treatment, access, opportunity, and advancement for all individuals while striving to identify and eliminate barriers that have prevented the full participation of some groups.

ECDI

Equity, Cultural Diversity, & Inclusion Competency (Also referred to as Inclusion Competency: a framework for organizational change that fosters a sustainable environment where inclusion, productivity, and engagement thrive among employees.

Equity

Equity refers to a condition where race no longer predicts a person's outcomes in areas like societal, community, and workplace opportunities. It involves identifying and eliminating systemic barriers, policies, and practices that have historically disadvantaged marginalized and excluded people, while also ensuring access to opportunities and resources to everyone. Unlike equality, which focuses on giving everyone the same resources, equity recognizes that different groups may need different levels of support, due to a history of marginalization and exclusion, to achieve fair outcomes because of unequal starting points and systemic disadvantages.

Fairness in racial equity means ensuring that everyone has what they need to succeed, acknowledging and addressing the historical and current factors that create unequal conditions, rather than treating everyone exactly the same. Creating fairness involves identifying and removing barriers to ensure equal opportunities for all individuals.

Executive Summary

A concise overview of a strategic plan's purpose, key goals, strategies, and expected outcomes, aimed at engaging stakeholders.

Focus Group

A group of people assembled to participate in a guided discussion about a particular topic for the purpose of gathering opinions and insights.

Historically Marginalized and Excluded Group (HMEG)

Historically marginalized and excluded group refers to a demographic with a long history of being systematically disadvantaged, discriminated against, or excluded from full participation in social, economic, and political life. These groups have faced long-standing barriers and inequities due to factors such as race, ethnicity, gender, sexual orientation, disability, or socioeconomic status. The document mentions several examples of historically marginalized groups, including Black, Indigenous, and People of Color (BIPOC), women, LGBTQIA+ individuals, and other HMEG (Historically Marginalized and Excluded Groups) members. These groups often encounter systemic barriers in areas such as employment, education, and healthcare, which perpetuate cycles of disadvantage and exclusion.

Historically Majority and Included Group (HMIG)

The term "historically included and majority group" (HMIG) refers to a social group that has historically held dominant status, access to institutional power, and cultural authority within a given society. In the context of the United States, White Americans are commonly referred to as the historically majority and included group because they have long constituted the demographic majority and have been institutionally included in the nation's economic, political, and social systems by default.

Inclusion

The practice of ensuring that people feel a sense of belonging and support within an organization allows them to participate fully.

Key Informant Interview

A qualitative research method involving in-depth interviews with people who have specialized knowledge about a particular topic.

Metrics and Key Performance Indicators

Metrics are quantitative measures that track various activities, processes, or outcomes within an organization. For example, they might include percentage of workforce diversity, total sales, the number of customers served, or the employee turnover rate. In contrast, Key Performance Indicators (KPIs) are a specific subset of metrics that focus on the most critical measures tied directly to an organization's strategic goals and priorities. While all KPIs are metrics, not all metrics are KPIs.

Metrics and KPIs work together by providing both broad and focused insight into organizational performance. Metrics offer a wide range of data across different areas, allowing leaders to monitor various aspects of operations. From these metrics, leaders identify the most important measures, or KPIs, that serve as key signals of progress toward strategic objectives. Essentially, metrics show everything that can be measured, while KPIs highlight the vital few that matter most for success. Metrics help track overall performance, while KPIs provide actionable insights into whether the organization is achieving its objectives and guide data-informed decision-making. If an organization performs better in areas with a high percentage of cultural diversity among team members compared to areas with lower percentages, the performance gaps can be identified along with the indicators.

Organizational Change

The process through which an organization changes its structure, strategies, operational methods, technologies, or organizational culture to effect change within the organization and the effects of these changes on the organization.

Strategic Continuous Improvement Plan

A dynamic process where DEI practitioners set long-term goals, priorities, and resource plans while embedding regular review, feedback, and adaptation. This approach ensures DEI strategies remain responsive, data-driven, and aligned with evolving organizational and societal needs, fostering a culture of continuous learning and inclusive progress.

Vision Statement

A declaration of an organization's long-term goals and aspirations, intended to guide decision-making and inspire stakeholders.

About the Author

Billy Vaughn, Ph.D., is an internationally recognized thought leader in equity, cultural diversity, and organizational transformation. As the founder of Diversity Training University International (DTUI. com), Dr. Vaughn has spent nearly three decades helping organizations integrate fairness, inclusion, and intercultural competency into their operations and culture. His practical philosophy, scholarly work, and practice approach equips leaders with actionable strategies to address structural inequities and foster inclusive cultures.

With a background in cultural cognitive psychology and a passion for social justice, Dr. Vaughn has advised Fortune 500 companies, government agencies, and academic institutions on building equitable systems that work. He is sought after as a keynote speaker, consultant, and executive coach, known for his candid insights and evidence-based approach.

In *Fairness Reimagined,* Dr. Vaughn introduces an innovative framework for rethinking how organizations approach fairness, not viewing it as a vague ideal, but as a measurable, skill-based competency that drives systemic change while managing risk. Through real-world case studies, strategic tools, and deeply human insights, he challenges readers to rethink performative DEI approaches and to embrace a transformative equity strategy.

Index

References

- Attoh, K. A. (2019). Rights in Transit: Public Transportation and the Right to the City in California's East Bay. Athens: University of Georgia Press.
- Biden, J. Jr. (2021, June 25). On Diversity, Equity, Inclusion, and Accessibility in the Federal Workforce. White House Briefing. Retrieved from https://www.whitehouse.gov/briefing-room/presidential-actions/2021/06/25/executive-order-on-diversity-equity-inclusion-and-accessibility-in-the-federal-workforce/.
- Callaham, S. (2024, April 25). A revolution is coming and it will change the workplace as we know it. Forbes.
- Chambers, E. G., Foulon, M., Handfield-Jones, H., Hankin, S. M., & Michaels III, E. G. (1998). The war for talent. The McKinsey Quarterly, (3), 44–57.
- Devine, P. G., Monteith, M. J., Zuwerink, J. R., & Elliot, A. J. (1991). "Prejudice with and without Compunction." Journal of Personality and Social Psychology, 60(6), 817-830.
- Eagly, A. H., & Karau, S. J. (2002). Role congruity theory of prejudice toward female leaders. Psychological Review, 109(3), 573-598.
- Faragher v. City of Boca Raton, 524 U.S. 775. (1998). Retrieved from https://supreme.justia.com/cases/federal/us/524/775/.
- Gomez, L. E., & Bernet, P. (2019). Diversity improves performance and outcomes. Journal of the National Medical Association, 111(4), 383–392. https://doi.org/10.1016/j.jnma.2019.01.006.
- Greiner, L., & R. Metzger (1983), Consulting to management. Prentice-Hall, New Jersey.
- Griffith, Erin, (2021, April). "A Reckoning Over Objectivity, Led by the Data." *The New York Times*, 30 April 2021, (https://www.nytimes.com/2021/04/30/technology/basecamp-37signals.html).
- Harvard Business Publishing Corporate Learning. (2021). Organizational diversity, inclusion, and belonging: 2021 pulse report.
- Johnston, W. B., & Packer, A. H. (1987). Workforce 2000: Work and workers for the twenty-first century. Hudson Institute.

- Katz, J. H., & Miller, F. A. (1995). The path from monocultural club to inclusive organization: A developmental process. OD Practitioner, 27(4), 14–19.
- Keena, A. (2025, March 8). Shareholders are showing signs of DEI fatigue as activists push for more votes. Yahoo! Finance. Retrieved from https://finance.yahoo.com/news/shareholders-are-showing-signs-of-dei-fatigue-as-activists-push-for-more-votes-140136546.html.
- Krupnik, M. J. (2023, December 5). Harvard President Claudine Gay testifies before Congress. Harvard Magazine. Retrieved from https://www.harvardmagazine.com/2023/12/harvard-president-claudine-gay-testifies-congress.
- Littler Mendelson P.C. (2025, February 26). 2025 Inclusion, Equity, and Diversity C-Suite Survey Report. https://www.littler.com/sites/default/files/2025_littler_csuite_survey_report.pdf.
- L'Oréal USA. (n.d.). L'Oréal USA recognized for diversity & inclusion best practices. L'Oréal. Retrieved August 23, 2023, from https://www.loreal.com/en/usa/news/commitments/loreal-usa-recognized-for-diversity--inclusion-best-practices/.
- McKinsey & Company. (2020). Diversity wins: How inclusion matters. Retrieved from https://www.mckinsey.com/featured-insights/diversity-and-inclusion/diversity-wins-how-inclusion-matters.
- McKinsey & Company. (2021). The Black experience at work in charts. McKinsey & Company: Featured Insights. Retrieved from URL: https://www.mckinsey.com/featured-insights/diversity-and-inclusion/the-black-experience-at-work-in-charts.
- National Urban League, 2005). Diversity Best Practices That Work: The American Worker Speaks. http://nul.stage.iamempowered.com/content/diversity-practices-work-american-worker-speaks.
- National Urban League. (2009). Diversity practices that work: The American worker speaks. New York: National Urban League.
- Pratto, F., Sidanius, J., & Levin, S. (2006). Social dominance theory and the dynamics of intergroup relations: Taking stock and looking forward. European Review of Social Psychology, 17(1), 271–320. https://doi.org/10.1080/10463280601055772.

- Rice, D., et al. (2025, February 20, with multiple authors listed in the appendix). DEI programs are lawful under federal civil rights laws and Supreme Court precedent. [Email].
- Rosenbaum, E. (2017, May). Wells Fargo — facing lawsuits about preying on minorities — just won a diversity award. CNBC. https://www.cnbc.com/2017/05/04/wells-fargo-amid-minority-targeting-lawsuits-wins-diversity-award.html.
- SHRM (Society for Human Resource Management). (2020). Report: Black and White Workers Diverge on Racial Inequity in American Workplaces. URL: https://www.shrm.org/about-shrm/press-room/press-releases/pages/report-black-and-white-workers-diverge-on-racial-inequity-in-american-workplaces.aspx.
- Sieghart, M. A. (2024, November 15). Too many women excel at their jobs but are ignored for top roles. Financial Times. https://www.ft.com/content/729d1a32-62bf-4d61-b3e3-0763b7fe93ca.
- Vaara, E., Harju, A., Leppälä, M. & Buffart, M., 2021. How to Successfully Scale a Flat Organization. Harvard Business Review. [online] Available at: https://hbr.org/2021/06/how-to-successfully-scale-a-flat-organization [Accessed 18 August 2023].
- Vaughn, B. E. (2008). The short-sighted Washington Post article about diversity training. DTUI.com Diversity Blog. http://dtui.com/diversityblog/14/.
- Vaughn, B. E. (2007). Strategic Diversity & Inclusion Management Magazine, pp. 11 – 16, Vol. 1, Issue 1, Spring 2007. DTUI.com Publications Division. https://diversityofficermagazine.com/diversity-inclusion/the-history-of-diversity-training-its-pioneers/
- Vaughn, B. E. (2002). A heuristic model of managing emotions in race relations training. In E. Davis-Russell (Ed.), The California School of Professional Psychology handbook of multicultural education, research, intervention, and training (pp. 296–318). Jossey-Bass/Wiley.

Resources

- Diversity Executive Leadership Academy (certification programs) -https://diversityexecutiveacademy.com
- DTUI.com Continuing Education Resources - https://continuingeducation.dtui.com
- DTUI.com – Consulting and Training services
- The ECDI Global Legal Forum [LinkedIn Group] - https://www.linkedin.com/groups/1286257/

www.ingramcontent.com/pod-product-compliance
Lightning Source LLC
Chambersburg PA
CBHW030405270326
41926CB00009B/1271